__The Absent Dad:__ Understanding the Impact on Your Daughter's Future

First Edition: October, 2024
ISBN: 9798343484908

Cover design by Cristen Weldon
Published by Skynet Agencies

Dedication

To the daughters who have walked the path of healing, and to the fathers who strive to rebuild their bonds.

This book is for those who seek to understand, to heal, and to find strength in their stories.
May you find the courage to move from absence to empowerment.

Acknowledgements

Writing this book has been a deeply personal journey, and it would not have been possible without the support of many people who have helped me along the way.

To my family and friends, thank you for your encouragement and understanding as I poured my heart into this work. Your unwavering belief in me kept me motivated throughout the writing process.

To the daughters who have shared their stories with me, your vulnerability and resilience have been a source of inspiration. This book would not exist without your willingness to trust me with your experiences.

I am also grateful to the many professionals in the field of psychology, therapy, and fatherhood studies who have provided insight and guidance. Your dedication to healing and helping others has shaped much of what is shared in these pages.

A special thanks to my editor for your keen eye and thoughtful feedback, and to my publisher, Skynet Agencies, for believing in this project and helping bring it to life.

Lastly, to anyone who picks up this book with the intention of healing, learning, or supporting a loved one: this is for you. Thank you for allowing me to be part of your journey.

Table of Contents

Introduction

A. Purpose of the Book

1) Overview of the psychological, emotional, and social effects of an absent father on daughters.

The journey of a daughter growing up without a father is often paved with complex emotions and experiences that shape her identity and worldview. This book aims to delve into the psychological, emotional, and social effects of an absent father on daughters, offering a comprehensive examination of how this absence influences their lives. By understanding the multifaceted impact of father absence, we can better appreciate the resilience of those affected and highlight the pathways to healing and empowerment.

Psychological Effects: The Weight of Absence

Psychologically, the absence of a father can create a profound sense of loss that reverberates throughout a daughter's life. **Research has consistently shown** that children thrive in environments where parental figures are present, offering guidance, support, and stability. Without a father, daughters often grapple with feelings of abandonment, leading to deep-seated issues such as **low self-esteem** and **identity confusion**. The internalization of these feelings can manifest as anxiety or depression, hindering emotional development and leading to difficulties in forming healthy relationships later in life.

The struggle to forge a self-identity becomes even more pronounced as daughters navigate their formative years. The absence of a father figure can result in a skewed perception of what relationships should look like, often leaving daughters to seek validation from peers or romantic partners. These relationships may be fraught with insecurity and fear of abandonment, mirroring the unresolved emotions stemming from their father's absence. As a result, many daughters find themselves caught in a cycle of seeking approval while simultaneously fearing intimacy, creating a complex psychological landscape that can be challenging to navigate.

Emotional Turmoil: The Search for Connection

Emotionally, daughters of absent fathers often experience a tumultuous journey marked by grief and longing. The heartache of not having a father present during critical milestones - such as graduations, weddings, and other rites of passage - can leave lasting scars. The **emotional void** created by this absence may lead to feelings of anger, resentment, or sadness. Daughters may wrestle with questions such as, "Why wasn't I enough for him to stay?" or "What's wrong with me?" These thoughts can plague their minds, shaping their emotional responses and self-image.

The impact of emotional turmoil can ripple through various aspects of life, affecting how daughters interact with others and perceive themselves. **In friendships,** they may struggle with trust and vulnerability, often erecting walls to shield themselves from further emotional pain. In romantic relationships, they might find themselves gravitating towards partners who replicate the father's absence, subconsciously reenacting patterns of abandonment and seeking out emotionally unavailable individuals. This cycle not only reinforces feelings of unworthiness but also perpetuates the cycle of emotional pain, making it challenging for daughters to break free and cultivate healthy, fulfilling relationships.

Social Implications: Navigating a World Without a Father

Socially, the absence of a father can lead to isolation and feelings of alienation. In a world that often romanticizes the traditional family structure, daughters may feel like outsiders, grappling with societal expectations that emphasize the importance of a father in a family unit. This can manifest in various ways, including difficulties in peer relationships and challenges in social settings. The **stigma** associated with being a "fatherless daughter" can create a barrier to forming connections with others who may not understand their unique experiences.

Moreover, the lack of a father figure can significantly impact a daughter's understanding of gender roles and relationships. In families where fathers are absent, daughters may find themselves looking to their mothers or other caregivers for guidance. While these relationships can be nurturing, they may lack the balance and perspective that a father figure could provide. Consequently, daughters may struggle to define their own identities as women, often feeling torn between the expectations imposed by society and their understanding of what it means to be a daughter without a father.

A Call for Understanding and Healing

As we embark on this exploration of the absent father effect on daughters, it is crucial to acknowledge the complexity of these experiences. This book seeks not only to illuminate the challenges faced by fatherless daughters but also to provide insights into the pathways of healing and growth. By shedding light on the psychological, emotional, and social ramifications of father absence, we aim to foster a deeper understanding of the unique journeys these daughters navigate. Ultimately, our goal is to empower readers to recognize their resilience, find solace in shared experiences, and cultivate healthier relationships with themselves and others. Through this exploration, we hope to inspire healing and growth, demonstrating that despite the weight of absence, there is always hope for a brighter future.

2) The Aim: Exploring the Lifelong Impact of Father Absence

The absence of a father can cast a long shadow over a daughter's life, influencing her development in ways that extend far beyond childhood. This book seeks to explore how this absence profoundly impacts various aspects of a daughter's life, from the early years of her upbringing to her adult relationships and self-perception. By examining the trajectory of a fatherless daughter, we aim to uncover the intricate layers of this experience, shedding light on both the challenges faced and the resilience developed in the face of adversity.

Childhood: Formative Years Marked by Absence

In childhood, the absence of a father can create a tumultuous emotional landscape for daughters. During these formative years, children rely heavily on their primary caregivers for guidance, support, and affection. The absence of a father figure often leads to feelings of abandonment and insecurity, which can manifest in a variety of ways. **Young girls may struggle with trust and attachment**, finding it challenging to form close relationships with peers. This struggle is compounded by the societal narrative that places great importance on paternal involvement, leading many fatherless daughters to question their self-worth and desirability.

In the classroom, the effects of father absence can be equally pronounced. Research indicates that children without involved fathers are more likely to experience difficulties in academic performance. The lack of a father's encouragement and guidance can result in lower self-esteem, diminishing their motivation to excel in school. Moreover, the emotional turmoil stemming from an absent father can lead to behavioral issues, such as acting out or withdrawing socially, further isolating these daughters from their peers. As they navigate their early years, the scars of paternal absence begin to shape their identities, often leaving them feeling unworthy of love and success.

Adolescence: Navigating the Storms of Self-Discovery

As daughters transition into adolescence, the impact of a father's absence can deepen, influencing their exploration of identity, sexuality, and relationships. This critical period of self-discovery is often fraught with challenges, and the absence of a father can exacerbate feelings of confusion and uncertainty. **In the realm of romantic relationships,** fatherless daughters may find themselves grappling with trust issues and a heightened fear of abandonment. Many may unconsciously seek out partners who mirror their father's absence - emotionally unavailable or neglectful - believing that these dynamics are normal and familiar.

During this phase, daughters often confront the realities of their father's absence more acutely. They may experience anger or resentment, questioning why their father chose to leave or why he was unable to be present in their lives. This emotional upheaval can lead to a rebellious phase, where the search for validation and love may drive them to engage in risky behaviors, including substance use or tumultuous relationships. As they seek to fill the void left by their father, these daughters may inadvertently put themselves in harm's way, complicating their already tumultuous path toward adulthood.

Adulthood: The Lingering Echoes of Father Absence

Entering adulthood, the consequences of growing up without a father can manifest in profound ways, shaping a daughter's relationships, career choices, and overall self-perception. The emotional scars of a father's absence can hinder personal and professional growth, often resulting in challenges in establishing healthy relationships with romantic partners, friends, and even colleagues. Adult daughters may find themselves continuously battling feelings of inadequacy, grappling with their self-worth, and struggling to articulate their needs in relationships. **The fear of vulnerability can create barriers**, making it difficult for them to experience deep connections with others.

In the workplace, the impact of a father's absence can also be felt. Daughters may carry a persistent fear of failure or criticism, stemming from a childhood where they lacked paternal support and affirmation. This can hinder their ambition and drive, causing them to question their abilities and potential. Furthermore, they may struggle with authority figures, echoing the unresolved conflicts from their past. The absence of a father may also influence their decision-making processes, as they grapple with issues of self-doubt and seek validation from others rather than trusting their instincts.

The Path to Healing and Empowerment

Despite these challenges, it is essential to recognize that fatherless daughters possess remarkable resilience. Through the exploration of their experiences, we aim to provide insights into how these daughters can reclaim their narratives and find empowerment in their journeys. While the absence of a father can create significant hurdles, it also opens the door to growth, self-discovery, and the ability to form meaningful connections on their own terms.

This book will serve as a guide for understanding the multifaceted effects of father absence while highlighting the paths toward healing and personal growth. By illuminating the struggles faced by fatherless daughters and offering practical strategies for overcoming these obstacles, we hope to inspire readers to embrace their identities, cultivate self-love, and foster healthier relationships. The journey may be fraught with challenges, but it is also filled with potential for transformation and empowerment, proving that even in the face of absence, strength and resilience can thrive.

B. Personal Stories & Case Studies

1) Introduction of Real-Life Stories: Illuminating the Father-Daughter Dynamic

To fully grasp the complex effects of an absent father on daughters, it is crucial to weave in real-life stories and case studies that illuminate the myriad ways this absence can shape their lives. These narratives provide invaluable insights into the emotional landscapes of fatherless daughters, showcasing the varied responses to paternal absence and the unique challenges they face. By exploring these personal stories, we can better understand the profound implications of father-daughter relationships and the resilience that often emerges from hardship.

Case Study 1: Sarah's Journey Through Anger and Forgiveness

Take, for instance, the story of Sarah, a 28-year-old woman who grew up in a single-parent household after her father left when she was just three years old. Throughout her childhood, Sarah felt an acute sense of loss, compounded by the emotional toll of her father's absence. She recalls moments of intense anger, particularly during significant life events such as her high school graduation and college acceptance, when she longed for her father's presence and support.

This absence manifested in her adolescent years as she struggled to forge connections with her peers, often pushing them away out of fear of being abandoned again. Sarah's early relationships were fraught with turmoil, as she unconsciously gravitated toward partners who replicated the emotional neglect she had experienced as a child. It wasn't until her mid-twenties that Sarah sought therapy to address her unresolved feelings. Through therapy, she began to unravel the layers of her anger and grief, ultimately finding a path toward forgiveness - not only for her father but for herself. This journey of self-discovery empowered Sarah to reclaim her narrative, allowing her to embrace her worthiness and cultivate healthier relationships moving forward.

Case Study 2: Mia's Struggle for Identity

Mia's story illustrates another facet of the absent father dynamic. At just 21 years old, Mia found herself grappling with identity and self-worth after her father walked out when she was ten. Growing up, she experienced an overwhelming sense of confusion about her own value, often believing she wasn't good enough to be loved. As she navigated her teenage years, Mia faced immense pressure to prove herself in academics and athletics, striving to earn the love and attention that had been absent from her father.

Despite her accomplishments, Mia felt a persistent void, often comparing herself to her friends who had their fathers present. The lack of a paternal figure created an identity crisis; she struggled to define herself outside of societal expectations and the shadows of her father's absence. The turning point for Mia came during her sophomore year of college when she joined a support group for fatherless daughters. Here, she discovered the power of shared experiences and began to forge connections with others who understood her struggles. Through these interactions, Mia began to reclaim her identity, realizing that her worth was not tied to her father's absence. Instead, she learned to appreciate her unique strengths and aspirations, ultimately transforming her narrative from one of loss to one of empowerment.

Case Study 3: Lisa's Quest for Connection

Lisa's narrative reflects the complex interplay between father absence and relationship dynamics. As a 35-year-old mother of two, Lisa grew up with an emotionally distant father who was physically present but rarely engaged in her life. The emotional disconnect left Lisa feeling unworthy and craving validation throughout her youth. She often found herself seeking approval from others, especially in romantic relationships, where she would compromise her own needs to maintain connections.

In her thirties, Lisa entered a series of tumultuous relationships, each mirroring the emotional unavailability she had experienced with her father. It wasn't until she became a mother that she confronted the lingering effects of her upbringing. Determined to break the cycle, Lisa sought therapy to understand her relationship patterns and emotional triggers. Through this process, she recognized the need to establish healthy boundaries and prioritize her own needs. By focusing on self-love and healing, Lisa began to cultivate a nurturing environment for her children, ensuring they would grow up feeling valued and supported. Her journey demonstrates that while father absence can create deep wounds, it can also spark a quest for connection and personal growth, ultimately allowing one to forge healthier family dynamics.

Case Study 4: Julia's Empowerment Through Activism

Julia's story highlights the empowering potential that can arise from father absence. Growing up in a tumultuous household after her father left, Julia was determined to rise above her circumstances. Instead of succumbing to the feelings of abandonment and inadequacy that often accompany paternal absence, Julia channeled her energy into activism and community service. By engaging with causes that resonated with her experiences - such as advocating for youth mentorship programs and fatherhood initiatives - Julia found purpose and meaning in her journey.

Her commitment to making a difference not only helped others but also facilitated her own healing. Through her work, Julia developed a strong sense of identity and community, proving that adversity can indeed be a catalyst for change. Her story serves as a testament to the resilience of fatherless daughters, illustrating how they can transform their pain into empowerment, leading to a life of purpose and connection.

The Power of Personal Narratives

These real-life stories illustrate the varied and profound impacts of father absence on daughters. They serve as powerful reminders that, while the absence of a father can leave indelible scars, it can also ignite journeys of healing, resilience, and personal growth. By highlighting these narratives, we aim to foster a deeper understanding of the complexities of father-daughter relationships, shedding light on the emotional landscapes that shape the lives of fatherless daughters. Through shared experiences, we can cultivate empathy and awareness, paving the way for healing and transformation in the lives of those affected by paternal absence.

C. Defining "Absent"

1) Clarifying the Types of Absence: Physical, Emotional, or Both

The term "absent" evokes a range of interpretations, particularly when applied to the complex father-daughter dynamic. While the most overt form of absence is physical - where a father is simply not present in the daughter's life - there exists a deeper, more nuanced understanding that encompasses emotional absence as well. It is essential to differentiate between these types of absence, as each carries distinct implications for the psychological and emotional well-being of daughters. By clarifying these categories, we can begin to unravel the multifaceted nature of father absence and its lasting effects on daughters throughout their lives.

Physical Absence: The Overt Void

Physical absence refers to the situation where a father is not present in a daughter's life, whether due to abandonment, divorce, death, or incarceration. This absence is often the most visible and immediate form of loss, creating a palpable void that impacts daily life. The emotional ramifications of physical absence can be profound, leading to feelings of rejection, abandonment, and worthlessness. For a daughter, the absence of a father during formative years can manifest as a constant question: *Why wasn't I enough for him to stay?*

The impact of physical absence often becomes evident during significant milestones - birthdays, graduations, and other life events - when daughters feel the weight of their father's absence acutely. These moments can serve as painful reminders of the love and support they yearn for but never received. Many daughters of absent fathers recount experiences of longing, where they fantasize about what their relationship with their father could have been. These feelings can lead to an ongoing cycle of grief, affecting their ability to form secure

12

attachments with others. Consequently, daughters may develop strategies to cope with this absence, sometimes leading to rebellious behavior or withdrawal, as they struggle to fill the void left by their father's departure.

Emotional Absence: The Invisible Strain

On the other hand, emotional absence refers to a father's lack of engagement, support, and affection, even when he is physically present. This type of absence can be equally, if not more, damaging than physical absence. A father who is physically present but emotionally unavailable creates an environment of confusion and insecurity for his daughter. She may witness his physical presence in the household, yet feel isolated and unloved due to his emotional detachment. This can lead to a deep-seated belief that she is unworthy of love or connection.

Emotional absence often manifests in the form of neglect, where a father may prioritize work, hobbies, or relationships outside the family over the emotional needs of his daughter. As a result, daughters may develop low self-esteem, believing they do not deserve attention or affection. This emotional neglect can have long-lasting effects on their mental health, influencing their self-worth and their ability to engage in healthy relationships in adulthood. Daughters may internalize feelings of inadequacy, perpetuating a cycle of emotional turmoil that can affect their personal and professional lives.

The Interplay of Physical and Emotional Absence

The most challenging scenario occurs when both physical and emotional absence intertwine. In such cases, daughters may experience a profound sense of abandonment that compounds the emotional distress of having a father who is neither physically nor emotionally available. This dual absence can lead to significant challenges in emotional regulation, often manifesting as anxiety, depression, or behavioral issues. The daughters of fathers who are both physically and emotionally absent may struggle to trust others, perpetuating a sense of isolation that can be difficult to escape.

Understanding the interplay between physical and emotional absence is crucial for recognizing the unique challenges faced by fatherless daughters. The absence of a father can lead to a lack of male role models, affecting daughters' perceptions of men and their expectations in relationships. The emotional scars of dual absence can shape their interactions, creating a ripple effect that extends beyond their immediate relationships. In many cases, these daughters may spend years navigating their pain, seeking closure and understanding as they strive to break free from the cycle of loss.

Moving Toward Healing: Acknowledging the Absence

Acknowledging the different forms of absence is an essential step toward understanding the profound effects on father-daughter relationships. By defining and exploring the nuances of physical and emotional absence, we can begin to appreciate the complexities of these experiences. This understanding paves the way for healing, allowing fatherless daughters to confront their past and embrace their identities. It also highlights the importance of nurturing healthy relationships and fostering emotional resilience, enabling them to move forward with strength and purpose.

In the chapters that follow, we will delve deeper into the specific ways these types of absence impact daughters' lives, from childhood through adulthood. Through personal stories, research, and insights, we aim to shed light on the profound implications of father absence, ultimately empowering readers to recognize and address the emotional scars that may linger from their experiences. As we journey through these narratives, we will uncover paths to healing and empowerment, reinforcing the idea that understanding and compassion can pave the way for a brighter future, even in the shadow of absence.

2) How Cultural, Economic, and Social Factors Contribute to Father Absence

Understanding the phenomenon of father absence requires a nuanced exploration of the various cultural, economic, and social factors that contribute to this issue. The interplay of these elements creates an environment where father absence can thrive, leaving a lasting impact on daughters and shaping their experiences in profound ways. By delving into these contributing factors, we can better appreciate the complexities surrounding father absence and its effects on family dynamics.

Cultural Influences: The Shifting Landscape of Fatherhood

Cultural attitudes towards fatherhood significantly shape the experiences of daughters who grow up without their fathers. In many societies, traditional gender roles dictate the expectations placed on men and women within family structures. These roles have evolved over the years, but certain cultural norms persist, influencing the perception of fatherhood and the responsibilities associated with it. In some cultures, the expectation for fathers to be the primary breadwinners can create a disconnect between their parental duties and their professional ambitions.

The rise of individualism in contemporary society has also altered the family dynamic, often prioritizing personal fulfillment over familial responsibilities. For instance, a father may choose to pursue career advancements or personal interests, leading to emotional detachment or physical absence. In cultures that de-emphasize the importance of fatherhood, the idea of a committed, nurturing father figure may be undermined, reinforcing patterns of absence. These cultural shifts can perpetuate cycles of disengagement, as daughters grow up with limited exposure to positive paternal role models, impacting their understanding of male relationships and their expectations for future partnerships.

Economic Factors: The Financial Strain on Families

Economic factors play a crucial role in father absence, often serving as a catalyst for familial disruption. Financial instability can lead to stress and conflict within households, prompting fathers to prioritize work over family life. In cases of economic hardship, some fathers may feel compelled to take on multiple jobs, leaving little time or energy for their daughters. This physical absence can be exacerbated by the emotional toll of financial strain, as fathers may become withdrawn or irritable, further distancing themselves from their families.

In addition, economic disparities can contribute to father absence in marginalized communities, where systemic issues such as poverty and unemployment create barriers to family stability. In these contexts, fathers may be incarcerated or face difficulties maintaining employment, leading to heightened rates of father absence. Daughters growing up in these environments often confront additional challenges, as they navigate the repercussions of their fathers' absence amid socioeconomic struggles. The cycle of poverty can perpetuate father absence, as daughters may internalize feelings of worthlessness or inadequacy, believing they are unworthy of a stable family environment.

Social Factors: The Influence of Family Structure and Support Systems

Social factors, including family structure and community support systems, also contribute to the prevalence of father absence. The rise of single-parent households has become increasingly common, often resulting from divorce or separation. In many cases, fathers may take on a less active role in their daughters' lives post-separation, either by choice or due to logistical challenges. The absence of a father figure can create emotional voids that daughters must navigate, leading to feelings of isolation and longing.

Moreover, societal attitudes toward single motherhood can influence the experiences of fatherless daughters. In cultures where stigma surrounds single-parent families, mothers may feel pressure to shield their children from the perceived shame of having an absent father. This can result in a lack of open discussion about the emotional impacts of father absence, preventing daughters from processing their feelings and experiences effectively. When community support systems are lacking, daughters may feel further isolated, unable to find the resources or guidance needed to address their emotional turmoil.

The Interconnectedness of Factors: A Complex Web of Absence

It is essential to recognize that these cultural, economic, and social factors do not exist in isolation. Instead, they intertwine to create a complex web of influences that contribute to father absence. For instance, a cultural expectation for fathers to be the primary providers may exacerbate economic strain, leading to emotional disengagement. Similarly, social stigma surrounding single-parent households can discourage open conversations about father absence, perpetuating feelings of isolation for daughters.

By examining these interconnected factors, we can better understand the multifaceted nature of father absence and its impact on daughters. Each factor contributes to a broader narrative of loss, shaping the emotional landscapes of fatherless daughters as they navigate their identities and relationships. Acknowledging these influences allows us to approach the issue of father absence with greater empathy and awareness, paving the way for more supportive resources and interventions.

The Importance of Understanding Contributing Factors

Cultural, economic, and social factors play a significant role in shaping the experiences of daughters who grow up without their fathers. By exploring these influences, we can deepen our understanding of the complexities surrounding father absence and its lasting impact on emotional well-being and relationships. Recognizing the interplay between these factors encourages a more holistic approach to addressing the issue, fostering resilience and empowerment among fatherless daughters. As we move forward in this exploration, we will delve into the specific effects of father absence on daughters' lives, seeking to illuminate pathways toward healing and connection.

Part 1: The Father-Daughter Bond and Its Importance

Chapter 1:

The Role of Fathers in Child Development

A. Exploring Traditional and Contemporary Roles of Fathers

The role of fathers in child development has undergone significant transformations over the years, reflecting broader societal changes in family dynamics, gender roles, and cultural expectations. Traditionally, fathers were often seen as the primary breadwinners, embodying a figure of authority and discipline in the household. Their role was largely confined to financial provision, leaving the nurturing and emotional upbringing of children primarily to mothers. However, contemporary perspectives on fatherhood have evolved, recognizing the crucial impact fathers have on the emotional, psychological, and social development of their daughters.

Traditional Roles: Authority and Provision

In traditional family structures, fathers were often viewed as the quintessential providers. They took on the role of the family's protector and economic backbone, working long hours to ensure financial stability. This approach established a clear hierarchy within the family unit, with fathers typically assuming the position of authority and decision-makers. Their interactions with their daughters were often limited to teaching discipline, instilling values, and modeling behaviors associated with success and responsibility.

While this model offered certain advantages, such as providing economic security, it often neglected the emotional needs of children, particularly daughters. The expectation for fathers to be strong and stoic frequently resulted in emotional distance, with fathers adopting a "tough love" approach. Daughters growing up in this environment may have experienced love and support through material means rather than emotional engagement, potentially leading to feelings of inadequacy or longing for deeper connections. As a result, many daughters learned to associate love with achievement or performance rather than genuine emotional closeness, shaping their future relationships and self-esteem.

The Evolution of Fatherhood: From Breadwinner to Nurturer

As society progressed through the latter half of the 20th century, the role of fathers began to shift dramatically. The feminist movement, alongside changes in economic conditions and family structures, prompted a reevaluation of traditional gender roles. With more women entering the workforce and pursuing careers, fathers were increasingly called upon to share parenting responsibilities. This transformation led to the emergence of the "hands-on" father - one who is actively involved in the day-to-day upbringing of his children.

Contemporary fathers are now recognized for their capacity to nurture and support their daughters emotionally. This involvement has been linked to numerous positive outcomes in child development, particularly in fostering healthy emotional well-being. Research has demonstrated that daughters with engaged fathers tend to exhibit higher self-esteem, better academic performance, and improved social skills. The emotional bond forged between a father and daughter plays a critical role in shaping her identity, self-worth, and ability to form healthy relationships in adulthood.

The Impact of Emotional Engagement: Building Resilience

Emotional engagement is paramount in father-daughter relationships, as it nurtures resilience and adaptability in daughters. Fathers who actively participate in their daughters' lives - attending school events, providing emotional support during challenging times, and engaging in open conversations - create a safe space for exploration and growth. This type of involvement allows daughters to develop a sense of security, knowing that their fathers are present and invested in their well-being.

Moreover, fathers who openly express affection and encouragement instill a sense of confidence in their daughters. They become vital role models, demonstrating how to navigate life's challenges with resilience and courage. Daughters who experience a loving and nurturing relationship with their fathers are more likely to approach life with optimism and self-assuredness, equipped with the skills to face adversity head-on. These daughters often learn the value of communication, empathy, and healthy emotional expression, skills that are essential for fostering positive relationships throughout their lives.

The Modern Father: Balancing Roles and Responsibilities

In the contemporary context, many fathers strive to balance the roles of provider, nurturer, and supporter. This multifaceted approach to fatherhood emphasizes the importance of being emotionally available while also fulfilling financial responsibilities. The modern father recognizes that his role extends beyond economic provision; he is also a critical influencer in his daughter's emotional and psychological development.

As fathers navigate the complexities of modern life, they face unique challenges, including societal pressures to conform to traditional gender roles and the demands of a fast-paced world. However, the shift towards shared parenting and involvement in children's lives has opened up new possibilities for fathers to connect with their daughters on a deeper level. By fostering open communication, engaging in shared activities, and showing unconditional love, modern fathers can help build strong, healthy relationships with their daughters, enabling them to thrive.

The Lifelong Impact of Fatherhood

The evolving roles of fathers in child development reflect significant shifts in societal attitudes and expectations. From traditional figures of authority to contemporary nurturers, fathers now play an essential role in shaping their daughters' emotional, psychological, and social landscapes. The presence of an engaged father can have profound effects, influencing daughters' self-esteem, resilience, and capacity for healthy relationships.

As we move forward in this exploration of the father-daughter bond, it is essential to recognize the lasting impact fathers have on their daughters' lives. By understanding the critical nature of their involvement, we can appreciate the importance of fostering strong, nurturing relationships that empower daughters to flourish in their personal and professional lives.

B. The Father-Daughter Relationship as a Cornerstone for Emotional Development

The father-daughter relationship is often viewed as one of the most significant dynamics in a young girl's life. This bond serves as a cornerstone for emotional development, influencing how daughters perceive themselves, relate to others, and navigate the complexities of their emotional worlds. Unlike any other relationship, the one between a father and daughter plays a crucial role in shaping a daughter's self-esteem, emotional intelligence, and overall mental health. The nuances of this relationship are vast, encompassing a wide range of emotions, interactions, and life lessons that collectively contribute to a daughter's emotional growth.

Building Self-Esteem Through Affirmation and Support

One of the most critical aspects of the father-daughter relationship is the impact it has on a daughter's self-esteem. Daughters with involved and affirming fathers often develop a strong sense of self-worth, grounded in the recognition and support they receive from their fathers. When fathers actively participate in their daughters' lives - whether through verbal affirmations, encouragement in their pursuits, or simply spending quality time together - they send a powerful message: "You are valued; you matter." This affirmation lays the groundwork for a daughter to develop a positive self-image.

The presence of a supportive father can counteract external criticisms and societal pressures that often plague young girls, particularly in today's world dominated by social media and unrealistic beauty standards. A father's praise can help daughters build resilience against these challenges, fostering a belief in their abilities and worthiness. In contrast, a lack of affirmation can lead to feelings of inadequacy, as daughters may internalize their fathers' absence or indifference as a reflection of their own value. Thus, the father-daughter relationship acts as a critical buffer against negative influences, enabling daughters to cultivate a healthier self-concept.

Emotional Intelligence: Navigating Complex Feelings

Fathers play an essential role in helping their daughters develop emotional intelligence, which encompasses the ability to understand, express, and manage emotions effectively. This skill is vital for building strong interpersonal relationships and navigating the challenges of life. When fathers engage in meaningful conversations with their daughters, encouraging them to express their feelings and thoughts openly, they model emotional awareness and regulation.

For instance, a father who listens attentively to his daughter's concerns and validates her feelings teaches her that emotions are not only normal but also important. This creates a safe space where daughters can explore their feelings without fear of judgment. As they grow, daughters learn to articulate their emotions, leading to healthier relationships with peers, family members, and future partners. Additionally, this foundation of emotional intelligence can significantly influence their problem-solving skills, empathy, and ability to cope with stress.

Modeling Healthy Relationships: Lessons in Love and Respect

The father-daughter relationship also serves as a powerful model for how daughters understand love, respect, and relationships. Fathers who demonstrate affection and respect towards their daughters provide a blueprint for what healthy relationships look like. Through their interactions, fathers can teach valuable lessons about boundaries, consent, and mutual respect - concepts that will be essential for daughters as they navigate friendships and romantic relationships later in life.

Conversely, daughters who experience neglect or emotional unavailability from their fathers may internalize unhealthy relational patterns, which can manifest in their future interactions. They might struggle with trust issues, fear of abandonment, or difficulties in establishing boundaries. The father-daughter dynamic, therefore, not only shapes immediate emotional responses but also influences long-term relationship patterns, illustrating the profound implications of this bond on a daughter's emotional landscape.

Resilience: A Lifelong Gift

One of the most enduring gifts a father can provide his daughter is resilience - the ability to bounce back from setbacks and navigate life's challenges. A strong father-daughter relationship fosters a sense of security that empowers daughters to face adversity with confidence. Fathers who encourage their daughters to take risks, learn from failures, and persevere in the face of challenges instill a growth mindset, enabling them to approach life's hurdles as opportunities for learning and growth.

This resilience is crucial, particularly during adolescence, a period marked by identity exploration and emotional upheaval. Daughters with supportive fathers are more likely to approach these turbulent years with a sense of self-assuredness, equipped with the skills to tackle obstacles head-on. The lessons learned from their fathers become integral to their emotional toolkit, enabling them to cope with life's uncertainties and pursue their goals fearlessly.

The Lasting Impact of the Father-Daughter Bond

The father-daughter relationship is more than just a familial bond; it is a foundational pillar for emotional development. Through affirmation, emotional intelligence, healthy relationship modeling, and resilience, fathers play a pivotal role in shaping their daughters' emotional landscapes. The effects of this relationship are profound and far-reaching, influencing not only how daughters view themselves but also how they navigate the world around them.

As we continue to explore the complexities of father-daughter dynamics in the following chapters, it becomes increasingly clear that the significance of this bond cannot be understated. Understanding the multifaceted nature of the father-daughter relationship provides insight into the emotional well-being of daughters and the essential role fathers play in nurturing their growth. By valuing and prioritizing this relationship, we can foster an environment where daughters flourish emotionally, paving the way for healthier relationships and a more empowered future.

C. Importance of Fathers in Establishing Boundaries, Self-Esteem, and Social Skills

The role of fathers in a child's development extends beyond mere companionship; it encompasses critical aspects of emotional and social growth. Fathers are instrumental in teaching their daughters about boundaries, fostering self-esteem, and developing essential social skills. The relationship between a father and daughter serves as a vital framework through which daughters learn how to navigate their world, understand their value, and establish healthy interactions with others.

Establishing Healthy Boundaries: A Crucial Lesson

Fathers play a pivotal role in helping daughters understand the concept of boundaries. Healthy boundaries are essential for emotional safety and personal identity. Through their interactions, fathers can model what it means to set and respect boundaries, which is vital for building relationships based on mutual respect and understanding.

When fathers demonstrate the importance of boundaries, they teach their daughters to recognize and articulate their own limits. This may manifest in everyday situations, such as learning to say "no" when uncomfortable, standing firm in personal beliefs, or understanding the significance of privacy. For instance, a father who actively listens when his daughter expresses discomfort in a social setting not only validates her feelings but also encourages her to assert her needs. This practice cultivates a sense of agency, empowering daughters to establish their own boundaries with peers, family members, and potential romantic partners.

Conversely, when fathers are absent or fail to respect boundaries, daughters may struggle to identify their limits, leading to confusion and potential vulnerabilities in their relationships. The absence of boundary-setting can result in a host of issues, including difficulty in

28

recognizing unhealthy relationships or tolerating disrespectful behavior. Thus, fathers not only provide a model for boundary-setting but also serve as protectors who reinforce their daughters' right to self-determination.

Fostering Self-Esteem: The Foundation of Self-Worth

The foundation of a daughter's self-esteem is often laid through the affirmations and support provided by her father. This self-esteem is essential for her emotional health, influencing how she perceives herself and her interactions with others. Fathers who actively participate in their daughters' lives - through praise, encouragement, and engagement - contribute to their sense of worthiness.

For instance, a father who celebrates his daughter's achievements, no matter how small, instills a belief in her capabilities. This affirmation can come in various forms: verbal praise, participation in her interests, or simply spending quality time together. These positive reinforcements help daughters cultivate a positive self-image, fostering resilience and a willingness to pursue their goals.

On the other hand, a lack of attention or affirmation from fathers can lead daughters to develop self-doubt and insecurity. They may internalize feelings of unworthiness, impacting their mental health and social interactions. This detrimental cycle can affect their relationships, as daughters may struggle to accept compliments or may constantly seek validation from others. Therefore, a father's role in fostering self-esteem cannot be overstated; it is a crucial component of a daughter's emotional development that reverberates throughout her life.

Developing Social Skills: Navigating Relationships

Fathers also significantly influence the development of social skills in their daughters. The interactions that take place within the father-daughter relationship serve as a training ground for navigating social dynamics. Through shared experiences - whether playing together, engaging in conversations, or facing challenges - fathers teach daughters essential skills such as communication, empathy, and conflict resolution.

Fathers who model healthy communication, actively listen, and engage in open discussions foster daughters who feel comfortable expressing themselves. This communicative environment encourages daughters to articulate their thoughts and feelings effectively, laying the groundwork for successful interactions with peers and authority figures. Furthermore, when fathers involve their daughters in activities that require teamwork or problem-solving, they provide opportunities for daughters to practice collaboration and negotiation.

Empathy, too, is an essential social skill that fathers can help cultivate. By demonstrating compassion and understanding in their interactions, fathers teach their daughters the importance of considering others' feelings and perspectives. A father who discusses the emotions behind a situation, such as a conflict with a friend, encourages his daughter to approach relationships with sensitivity and awareness.

The Ripple Effect: Long-Term Implications

The lessons imparted by fathers regarding boundaries, self-esteem, and social skills extend far beyond childhood. These foundational elements influence how daughters approach relationships throughout their lives. A daughter who learns to assert her boundaries and values her self-worth is more likely to seek out and maintain healthy relationships in adulthood. Similarly, those equipped with strong social skills are better prepared to navigate the complexities of the workplace and interpersonal dynamics.

Moreover, the positive impact of an involved father can create a ripple effect within families and communities. Daughters who are nurtured and supported are more likely to become nurturing and supportive parents themselves, perpetuating healthy relationship dynamics across generations. This continuity fosters environments where emotional well-being is prioritized, contributing to stronger, more resilient communities.

The Transformative Power of a Father's Influence

The role of fathers in establishing boundaries, fostering self-esteem, and developing social skills is profound and transformative. Fathers serve as essential figures in their daughters' lives, providing guidance and modeling behaviors that shape their emotional and social development. By prioritizing these aspects of their relationship, fathers empower their daughters to navigate the complexities of life with confidence and resilience.

As we continue to explore the significance of the father-daughter bond, it becomes increasingly clear that the lessons learned in childhood will echo throughout a daughter's life. Understanding the importance of a father's influence provides insight into the broader implications of this relationship, highlighting the necessity of nurturing these bonds for the sake of emotional well-being and personal growth. The journey of a daughter, shaped by her father's involvement, is one of empowerment, resilience, and ultimately, the ability to thrive in a complex world.

Chapter 2:

The Impact of a Present Father

A. The Positive Influence of a Present, Engaged Father on a Daughter's Emotional Health

A father's presence in a daughter's life is a profound determinant of her emotional health and overall well-being. The influence of an engaged father goes beyond superficial interactions; it penetrates the core of a daughter's emotional landscape, shaping her sense of security, identity, and interpersonal relationships. The nurturing bond created through consistent presence and involvement offers myriad benefits that contribute to a daughter's resilience, confidence, and ability to navigate life's challenges.

The Foundation of Emotional Security

At the heart of a healthy father-daughter relationship lies the foundation of emotional security. A present father provides a safe space for his daughter to explore her feelings, thoughts, and fears without judgment. This emotional safety net fosters an environment where daughters feel free to express themselves, knowing they will be heard and understood.

For example, when a daughter feels comfortable sharing her concerns or disappointments with her father, she is more likely to process her emotions constructively. This open communication establishes a crucial emotional framework, allowing her to develop healthy coping mechanisms. In contrast, a lack of paternal presence may lead to feelings of neglect or insecurity, making it difficult for daughters to openly express themselves or seek support when faced with challenges. Thus, a father's engagement is vital in fostering an environment where emotional expression is valued and encouraged.

Building Resilience Through Support

Engaged fathers also play an essential role in cultivating resilience in their daughters. The challenges of life can be daunting, and having a father who is present and supportive can significantly bolster a daughter's ability to cope with adversity. A father's encouragement during difficult times not only reinforces a daughter's belief in her abilities but also provides her with valuable tools for overcoming obstacles.

Fathers can teach their daughters how to approach challenges with a problem-solving mindset. For instance, a father who actively participates in his daughter's extracurricular activities - be it sports, academics, or arts - demonstrates the importance of perseverance. By providing constructive feedback and celebrating her achievements, he instills in her a sense of competence and determination. This supportive presence nurtures a daughter's ability to face challenges head-on, fostering resilience that will serve her throughout her life.

Furthermore, the experiences shared between a father and daughter during times of hardship can deepen their emotional bond. Whether it's navigating the complexities of a difficult school project or dealing with the loss of a loved one, these shared experiences teach daughters that they are not alone in facing life's challenges. The support of a present father during trying times becomes a cornerstone of their emotional development, teaching them that seeking help and relying on loved ones is a sign of strength, not weakness.

Enhancing Self-Esteem and Self-Identity

The involvement of a father significantly impacts a daughter's self-esteem and sense of self-identity. A present father actively engages in his daughter's interests, dreams, and aspirations, providing her with the validation and affirmation she needs to believe in herself. This positive reinforcement cultivates a strong sense of self-worth, which is essential for her emotional health and overall development.

For instance, when a father takes an interest in his daughter's hobbies - whether it be art, sports, or academics - he not only validates her passions but also encourages her to pursue them with enthusiasm. A father who expresses pride in his daughter's achievements, no matter how small, fosters a sense of accomplishment that boosts her confidence. This dynamic builds a foundation of self-esteem that allows her to tackle challenges with assurance and a belief in her abilities.

In contrast, a lack of paternal engagement can lead to self-doubt and insecurity. Daughters who grow up without a supportive father figure may struggle with their self-image and seek external validation from peers or others, often leading to unhealthy comparisons or feelings of inadequacy. Therefore, a present father plays a crucial role in helping his daughter forge a positive self-identity and an unwavering belief in her worth.

The Role of Positive Modeling in Relationships

A father's influence extends beyond the emotional realm; it also serves as a crucial model for future relationships. A present father sets the standard for how his daughter perceives male figures in her life. Through his actions, he teaches her what respect, love, and healthy communication look like in relationships.

For instance, a father who treats his daughter's mother (or any significant female figure in her life) with kindness and respect exemplifies the behaviors that his daughter will seek in her future relationships. When a father engages in open and honest communication, he illustrates the importance of transparency and vulnerability. This modeling can lead daughters to develop healthier expectations for their interactions with men, recognizing the value of mutual respect and understanding.

Additionally, fathers who encourage their daughters to engage with a diverse range of people - be it friends, family, or mentors - help them understand the importance of empathy, connection, and cooperation. These lessons create a solid foundation for emotional intelligence, allowing daughters to navigate interpersonal relationships with grace and confidence.

Long-Term Emotional Benefits

The long-term emotional benefits of having a present father are profound and far-reaching. Daughters who experience an engaged father figure are more likely to develop strong emotional regulation skills, fostering resilience in adulthood. They often find it easier to navigate complex social dynamics, build supportive networks, and manage stress effectively.

Moreover, the security and self-esteem instilled by a present father contribute to healthier relationships as daughters transition into adulthood. They tend to choose partners who mirror the respect and support modeled by their fathers, leading to more fulfilling and stable romantic relationships. The emotional toolkit developed through this relationship enhances their overall quality of life, enabling them to pursue their goals and dreams with confidence.

The Transformative Power of a Present Father

The impact of a present, engaged father on a daughter's emotional health cannot be overstated. From establishing emotional security and fostering resilience to enhancing self-esteem and modeling healthy relationships, the benefits of an involved father resonate throughout a daughter's life. By actively participating in their daughters' lives, fathers create a nurturing environment that empowers them to thrive emotionally and socially.

As we delve deeper into the nuances of father-daughter relationships, the importance of father presence remains a compelling theme. The positive influence of a father is a testament to the transformative power of engaged parenting, shaping daughters into confident, resilient individuals ready to face the complexities of life. The legacy of a present father is one that extends beyond the immediate family, nurturing future generations and fostering a culture of emotional well-being and healthy relationships.

B. Case Studies of Daughters with Involved Fathers

The impact of an involved father on a daughter's emotional and psychological development can be illuminated through real-life case studies. These narratives provide insight into how active paternal participation shapes daughters' lives, influences their choices, and bolsters their overall emotional health. By examining these diverse stories, we can better understand the profound implications of father involvement.

Case Study 1: Emily and Her Supportive Dad

Emily, a spirited twelve-year-old with a penchant for art, illustrates the profound influence of her father's active participation in her life. Her father, David, made a conscious decision to prioritize family time despite the demands of his career. Every Saturday, David and Emily dedicated time to explore art galleries, attend workshops, and engage in creative projects at home. This regular bonding not only nurtured Emily's artistic skills but also instilled in her a sense of self-worth and creativity.

David's encouragement of Emily's artistic endeavors allowed her to develop her identity as an artist. He actively showcased her work at local exhibitions and involved her in community art projects, reinforcing the belief that her voice mattered. When Emily faced challenges in school or personal life, she turned to her father for support, knowing he would listen without judgment. David's consistent presence fostered a strong emotional bond that encouraged Emily to express her feelings openly.

This case illustrates how an involved father can create a nurturing environment where daughters feel empowered to explore their passions and develop their identities. Emily's self-esteem flourished under her father's supportive guidance, proving that active engagement in a daughter's interests can profoundly influence her emotional landscape.

Case Study 2: Mia's Academic Journey

Mia, a high school senior with aspirations of becoming a scientist, presents another compelling case study. Her father, Richard, played an instrumental role in her academic journey. From a young age, Richard emphasized the importance of education and curiosity. He often engaged Mia in discussions about scientific concepts and took her on trips to science museums, sparking her interest in the field.

As Mia progressed through her studies, she encountered challenges, especially in advanced mathematics. Richard was not just a bystander; he became her tutor, dedicating evenings to help her grasp complex concepts. His patience and encouragement transformed Mia's frustration into resilience. When she faced setbacks, Richard reminded her that challenges were opportunities for growth, fostering a mindset that valued perseverance.

The results were remarkable. Mia graduated at the top of her class and received multiple scholarships to prestigious universities. She attributes much of her success to her father's unwavering support and belief in her capabilities. This case underscores how an involved father not only enhances a daughter's academic performance but also builds her resilience and problem-solving skills.

Case Study 3: Sarah and the Importance of Emotional Connection

Sarah, a twenty-five-year-old who now works as a mental health counselor, provides a poignant perspective on the emotional connection fostered by her father, Thomas. From her childhood, Thomas demonstrated the importance of emotional intelligence. He made it a priority to discuss feelings openly at home, ensuring that Sarah understood the value of expressing her emotions.

One pivotal moment occurred when Sarah faced bullying in middle school. Instead of dismissing her concerns or minimizing the situation, Thomas created a safe space for her to share her experiences. He listened intently, validating her feelings and helping her brainstorm strategies to cope with the bullying. This emotional support laid the groundwork for Sarah's understanding of healthy emotional expression, which later translated into her career in counseling.

Now, as a mental health professional, Sarah often reflects on her father's teachings. She emphasizes the importance of emotional vulnerability in her practice, helping her clients understand that it is both natural and healthy to express feelings. This case study illustrates the long-lasting impact of a father who prioritizes emotional connection, showcasing how such a relationship can shape a daughter's future interactions and professional choices.

Case Study 4: Jessica's Healthy Relationship Choices

Jessica, a thirty-year-old marketing executive, presents an interesting perspective on how her father's involvement influenced her romantic relationships. Her father, Michael, modeled respect and kindness in his marriage to Jessica's mother, which profoundly shaped Jessica's expectations in her own relationships. Growing up, she observed her father's supportive demeanor and commitment, which taught her the significance of mutual respect and communication.

During her teenage years, Jessica navigated several friendships and romantic relationships. When she faced challenges, she often turned to her father for advice. Michael encouraged her to seek partners who valued her as an individual, reinforcing the idea that love should be rooted in respect and kindness. This guidance empowered Jessica to set healthy boundaries and make choices that prioritized her well-being.

As an adult, Jessica has cultivated fulfilling relationships marked by open communication and respect, echoing the values instilled by her father. This case illustrates how a present father can serve as a positive role model, influencing his daughter's relationship choices and helping her build a healthy understanding of love and partnership.

The Lasting Impact of Father Involvement

These case studies illuminate the diverse ways in which present fathers positively influence their daughters. Whether through fostering creativity, enhancing academic success, promoting emotional intelligence, or modeling healthy relationship choices, engaged fathers play a pivotal role in shaping their daughters' lives. The common thread among these narratives is the profound emotional bond established through active participation and support.

In examining these stories, it becomes clear that the legacy of a present father extends far beyond childhood; it shapes daughters into resilient, confident individuals capable of navigating life's complexities. The power of a father's involvement is not merely an aspect of their upbringing but a transformative force that resonates throughout their lives, influencing their self-esteem, emotional health, and interpersonal relationships. As we continue to explore the father-daughter bond, these narratives underscore the immeasurable value of a present father in fostering a daughter's overall well-being and success.

C. Benefits in Terms of Confidence, Academic Performance, and Emotional Resilience

The presence of a father in a daughter's life can lead to remarkable benefits that resonate throughout her personal and academic development.

Confidence: The Foundation of Self-Worth

Confidence is a cornerstone of a daughter's development, and a present father plays an essential role in cultivating this vital attribute. From a young age, fathers contribute to their daughters' self-esteem through affirmation and encouragement. When a father actively participates in his daughter's life, offering praise for her achievements - big and small - he sends a powerful message that she is capable and valued. This affirmation is especially significant during formative years when children are forming their self-concepts.

Research indicates that girls who grow up with involved fathers tend to exhibit higher levels of self-confidence compared to those with absent fathers. This confidence manifests in various ways, including willingness to engage in new experiences, take on challenges, and assert themselves in social situations. A present father provides a safe space for daughters to express their thoughts and feelings, which further nurtures their self-worth. For instance, during family discussions, a father's validation of his daughter's opinions reinforces her belief that her voice matters, enhancing her sense of agency.

Moreover, the role of a father as a protector and guide fosters a sense of security in daughters. When they feel secure in their relationship with their father, daughters are more likely to step outside their comfort zones and explore new opportunities. This was notably evident in the case of Mia, who pursued her dream of becoming a scientist largely due to her father's unwavering belief in her abilities. Mia's confidence blossomed, allowing her to approach challenges with a proactive mindset.

Academic Performance: The Catalyst for Success

A father's involvement in his daughter's education can serve as a catalyst for academic success. Studies show that girls with engaged fathers often perform better academically than their peers with absent fathers. This performance can be attributed to several factors, including increased motivation, enhanced problem-solving skills, and the development of a strong work ethic.

Active participation in education, whether through help with homework, attending school events, or fostering a conducive learning environment at home, sends a clear message about the value of education. Fathers who prioritize learning create a culture of achievement within the household. For instance, Richard, who actively tutored his daughter Mia through challenging subjects, not only improved her understanding of mathematics but also instilled in her a sense of responsibility toward her studies.

Furthermore, the emotional support provided by an involved father can alleviate academic pressures. When daughters know they have someone to turn to for help, they are less likely to experience anxiety about schoolwork. This emotional security allows them to focus on their studies and perform to the best of their abilities. The relationship between a father and daughter fosters a growth mindset, where challenges are viewed as opportunities for learning rather than insurmountable obstacles.

Emotional Resilience: Bouncing Back from Adversity

Emotional resilience - the ability to adapt and thrive in the face of adversity - is another critical benefit of having a present father. Fathers who engage with their daughters emotionally equip them with essential coping mechanisms. They teach their daughters how to manage stress, process emotions, and confront challenges head-on, thus cultivating a robust emotional toolkit.

Daughters of involved fathers often develop greater emotional intelligence, allowing them to navigate relationships and social situations with empathy and understanding. This is largely because fathers who model emotional openness create a safe space for their daughters to express their feelings. When Thomas guided his daughter Sarah through difficult emotions during her bullying experience, he not only provided comfort but also modeled effective emotional processing. As a result, Sarah learned how to articulate her feelings and develop strategies to cope with adversity.

Moreover, the relationship between a father and daughter can serve as a blueprint for future relationships. Daughters with present fathers are more likely to seek healthy, supportive connections in adulthood. They have learned the importance of communication and mutual respect, making them better equipped to handle interpersonal challenges. This emotional resilience is not only beneficial in personal relationships but also plays a critical role in professional settings, where resilience and adaptability are key to success.

The Lasting Impact of a Present Father

The benefits of having an engaged father are multifaceted, profoundly influencing a daughter's confidence, academic performance, and emotional resilience. Through consistent support and active involvement, fathers foster an environment that promotes self-worth, encourages educational achievement, and develops emotional coping skills.

As daughters navigate the complexities of life, the foundation laid by their fathers becomes increasingly apparent. The lessons learned, the confidence instilled, and the emotional tools acquired shape their identities and equip them to face future challenges. Ultimately, the impact of a present father extends beyond childhood; it shapes daughters into empowered individuals capable of forging their paths and contributing positively to the world around them. As we continue to explore the intricacies of the father-daughter bond, it is essential to recognize the profound significance of paternal involvement in fostering healthy, resilient, and confident women.

Chapter 3:

Psychological and Emotional Effects

A. Increased Risks of Anxiety, Depression, and Emotional Neglect

The absence of a father figure during childhood can have profound psychological and emotional repercussions for daughters, significantly impacting their development and mental health. This chapter explores the increased risks of anxiety, depression, and emotional neglect that can arise from father absence, shedding light on the complexities of these issues and their long-lasting effects on young women.

The Shadow of Anxiety: A Lingering Presence

Anxiety disorders are among the most common mental health issues faced by children, and studies indicate that daughters who grow up without a father figure are at a heightened risk of developing these disorders. The absence of a paternal presence can create feelings of insecurity and instability, often leading to chronic anxiety that permeates various aspects of a child's life.

For instance, girls without engaged fathers may struggle with feelings of abandonment, which can trigger excessive worry about future relationships and experiences. The fear of being let down becomes a self-fulfilling prophecy, resulting in withdrawal from social situations and an inability to form healthy attachments. This was true for Jenna, who, having grown up without her father, often found herself paralyzed by the fear of rejection. This anxiety manifested in her reluctance to engage with peers, causing isolation and exacerbating her feelings of loneliness.

Research suggests that the emotional landscape of children is heavily influenced by their relationships with their parents. Daughters who experience father absence may internalize their feelings of loss and anxiety, often viewing the world through a lens of mistrust and uncertainty. As a result, they may find themselves trapped in a cycle of anxiety, which can lead to physical symptoms such as headaches, stomachaches, and fatigue. Understanding this connection between father absence and anxiety is crucial in developing effective interventions and support systems for affected children.

The Weight of Depression: An Overwhelming Burden

The emotional toll of father absence can extend beyond anxiety to include significant risks of depression. Studies indicate that daughters who lack a present father are more susceptible to developing depressive symptoms during childhood and adolescence. The feelings of inadequacy and unworthiness that often accompany a father's absence can lead to a pervasive sense of hopelessness, adversely affecting a child's emotional well-being.

Depression in children can manifest in various ways, including persistent sadness, irritability, and a loss of interest in activities once enjoyed. For example, Mia, who experienced her father's absence from an early age, began to withdraw from her favorite hobbies and friends as she entered her teenage years. The weight of her emotions became too heavy to bear, resulting in a downward spiral of despair. Her academic performance suffered, and she struggled to maintain friendships, ultimately leading to a deep-seated depression that required professional intervention.

Moreover, the stigma surrounding mental health can further complicate the experience of daughters who are depressed due to father absence. Many may feel ashamed of their feelings and, as a result, may be less likely to seek help or confide in others. This silence only deepens their struggle, creating a feedback loop where the absence of support compounds the emotional turmoil. Recognizing the signs of depression and providing adequate support can help daughters navigate these challenging waters, promoting healing and resilience.

Emotional Neglect: The Silent Epidemic

In addition to the psychological effects of anxiety and depression, father absence often results in emotional neglect, a form of maltreatment that can have severe consequences for a child's emotional development. Emotional neglect occurs when a child's emotional needs are consistently unmet, leading to feelings of invisibility, inadequacy, and worthlessness. For daughters, the absence of a father can create an emotional void that leaves them yearning for connection and affirmation.

The absence of paternal support can lead to a lack of emotional validation, leaving daughters struggling to understand and process their feelings. This neglect can hinder their ability to develop healthy emotional responses and coping mechanisms, making them vulnerable to future relational challenges. For instance, Sarah, whose father left when she was a toddler, often felt disconnected from her emotions. Lacking the guidance of a father who could help her navigate her feelings, she found herself unsure of how to express joy, sadness, or frustration. This emotional neglect not only affected her self-image but also impacted her relationships with others, creating a barrier to intimacy and trust.

Moreover, emotional neglect can have ripple effects that extend into adulthood. Women who experience emotional neglect in childhood may struggle with forming secure attachments, often gravitating toward unhealthy relationships that mirror their early experiences. They may find themselves in cycles of seeking approval from others while simultaneously fearing rejection. This pattern can perpetuate feelings of loneliness and isolation, leading to a complex web of emotional distress that can take years to unravel.

The Importance of Awareness and Intervention

Understanding the psychological and emotional effects of father absence is crucial in addressing the needs of affected daughters. Raising awareness about the risks of anxiety, depression, and emotional neglect can pave the way for early intervention and support. By providing resources and fostering open dialogues about mental health, communities can help daughters navigate their emotional challenges and build resilience.

Additionally, therapy and counseling can be invaluable tools in helping daughters process their feelings surrounding their father's absence. Engaging in therapeutic practices can empower them to develop healthier coping mechanisms, address their emotional needs, and forge positive relationships with themselves and others. With the right support, daughters can learn to overcome the psychological hurdles posed by father absence, reclaiming their narratives and building fulfilling lives.

Embracing Hope and Healing

The effects of father absence on daughters can manifest in increased risks of anxiety, depression, and emotional neglect, leaving lasting marks on their psychological and emotional well-being. However, understanding these challenges is the first step toward healing. By recognizing the significance of paternal involvement in shaping a daughter's emotional landscape, we can foster environments that support healthy development and resilience.

As we navigate the complexities of father absence, it becomes evident that hope and healing are possible. With awareness, intervention, and support, daughters can rise above the shadows cast by their fathers' absence, emerging as empowered individuals ready to confront the world with confidence, strength, and resilience. Through shared stories and compassionate understanding, we can break the cycle of silence and emotional neglect, paving the way for a brighter future for daughters everywhere.

B. Feelings of Abandonment, Rejection, and Unworthiness

The emotional landscape of a daughter raised without the presence of a father is often marred by complex feelings of abandonment, rejection, and unworthiness. These feelings can manifest in various ways, shaping a young woman's perception of herself and her relationships with others. Understanding the origins and implications of these feelings is crucial for addressing the emotional scars that may persist long into adulthood.

The Echo of Abandonment

Feelings of abandonment are among the most profound and distressing emotions experienced by daughters with absent fathers. The absence itself can create an emotional void that leaves daughters grappling with an overwhelming sense of loss. This loss may not only be physical but also emotional and psychological. A father's absence can lead to an inner narrative that suggests, "I was not important enough for him to stay," instilling a fear of being unlovable or unworthy.

For instance, consider the story of Lily, a young woman whose father left when she was just three years old. As she grew older, Lily found herself haunted by the belief that her father's departure was a reflection of her worth. Each time she encountered a relationship ending or a friend drifting away, the echoes of abandonment would surface, amplifying her fears of rejection. This internal struggle often led her to self-sabotage in friendships and romantic relationships, as she unconsciously anticipated being abandoned again.

The emotional ramifications of such abandonment can be profound. It fosters a pervasive anxiety that influences a daughter's interactions with others, causing her to remain guarded or overly dependent on those she allows into her life. The fear of further abandonment can lead to the avoidance of deep connections, trapping her in a cycle of loneliness and insecurity.

The Weight of Rejection

Rejection often follows closely behind feelings of abandonment, serving to reinforce the belief that one is unworthy of love and affection. Daughters with absent fathers frequently interpret their father's departure as a form of rejection, internalizing this message as a reflection of their value as individuals. This can manifest in a chronic fear of rejection in various aspects of life, including friendships, academics, and romantic endeavors.

Take, for example, Sarah, who constantly felt like an outsider among her peers. Growing up without her father, she often believed that she was inherently flawed. Her sense of worth was deeply tied to her father's absence; she wondered if he had chosen to leave because there was something wrong with her. This belief bled into her relationships, where she would often hold back from fully investing in friendships, fearing that if she allowed herself to be vulnerable, she would inevitably face rejection.

This fear can create a self-fulfilling prophecy. In avoiding emotional connections, daughters may inadvertently push people away, confirming their worst fears about rejection. This cycle perpetuates feelings of isolation and loneliness, further entrenching their belief that they are unworthy of love and companionship.

The Burden of Unworthiness

Perhaps the most insidious effect of father absence is the sense of unworthiness that can pervade a daughter's self-perception. This feeling often stems from a combination of abandonment and rejection. When a father is absent, a daughter may internalize the idea that she is not deserving of a father's love and attention. This belief can be so ingrained that it manifests as low self-esteem and self-worth, affecting every aspect of her life.

Consider the case of Emma, who grew up feeling like an afterthought. With her father's absence, she often compared herself unfavorably to her peers who had present fathers, leading her to believe that she was somehow less deserving of happiness and success. This belief became a barrier to her aspirations, causing her to shy away from opportunities that could enhance her self-worth. When she received praise or recognition, she found it difficult to accept, often attributing her achievements to luck rather than her own capabilities.

The implications of feeling unworthy can be far-reaching. It can hinder a daughter's ability to pursue goals, build healthy relationships, and advocate for herself. Daughters may become trapped in a cycle of self-doubt and self-criticism, convinced that they are not deserving of love, success, or happiness. This internalized unworthiness can have long-term consequences, often impacting their mental health and overall quality of life.

Healing the Emotional Wounds

Acknowledging and addressing feelings of abandonment, rejection, and unworthiness is crucial for the emotional healing of daughters who have experienced father absence. Recognizing these feelings is the first step toward reclaiming their narrative and fostering resilience. Through therapy and support, daughters can begin to untangle the complex web of emotions surrounding their father's absence and work towards healing.

Therapeutic practices can provide a safe space for daughters to explore their feelings and develop healthier self-perceptions. Cognitive-behavioral therapy (CBT), for instance, can help individuals challenge and reframe negative thought patterns that stem from feelings of unworthiness. Additionally, support groups can offer a sense of community and understanding, allowing daughters to share their experiences and learn from one another.

Encouraging self-compassion and self-acceptance can also play a vital role in healing. By learning to treat themselves with kindness and understanding, daughters can begin to shift their perspective on their worth. Engaging in activities that foster a sense of accomplishment and connection can further bolster their self-esteem, helping them build a more positive self-image.

The Path to Empowerment

Feelings of abandonment, rejection, and unworthiness are common among daughters who grow up without a father figure. These emotions can shape their identities, influencing their relationships and mental health. However, understanding the roots of these feelings is essential for healing and empowerment.

Through awareness, intervention, and support, daughters can learn to navigate their emotional challenges and reclaim their sense of worth. By breaking the cycle of pain and fostering resilience, they can forge a path toward a brighter future - one where they recognize their inherent value and embrace the possibility of love, connection, and belonging. As they heal, daughters can transform their narratives from that of abandonment to one of strength, resilience, and empowerment.

C. The Search for Approval and Validation in Other Male Figures

The absence of a father can create a profound void in a daughter's emotional landscape, prompting her to seek approval and validation from other male figures in her life. This quest for affirmation is not merely a desire for attention; it is an essential search for connection and identity in a world that may feel devoid of paternal support. Understanding the implications of this search and the dynamics that come into play is crucial for appreciating how father absence can shape a daughter's development.

The Need for Validation

Daughters who grow up without fathers often experience a deep-seated need for validation from male figures. This need arises from the emotional gap left by their father's absence, leading to an instinctive desire to fill that void. Without a father's affirming presence, daughters may feel insecure about their self-worth, viewing their value as contingent upon the recognition and approval of others, particularly men.

Take the story of Mia, a young woman who grew up with an absent father. Throughout her childhood, she found herself gravitating toward male teachers, mentors, and even older friends, seeking their praise and acknowledgment. Mia's self-esteem fluctuated dramatically based on the feedback she received from these figures. If a teacher praised her for her hard work, she would feel on top of the world, but a lack of acknowledgment would send her spiraling into feelings of inadequacy. This constant search for validation became a defining aspect of her emotional development, influencing her relationships and decision-making processes.

The need for validation can manifest in various forms, including the pursuit of romantic relationships with older partners, where the daughter may unconsciously seek out a father figure. In such cases, the daughter may project her unresolved feelings onto these relationships, leading to a dynamic where she feels dependent on her partner for approval and worthiness.

Complicated Dynamics with Male Figures

The search for approval often leads daughters to develop complex relationships with male figures, resulting in a blend of admiration, dependency, and sometimes, disappointment. In their pursuit of validation, daughters may idealize these figures, attributing to them qualities they wished to see in their absent fathers. This idealization can create unrealistic expectations, leading to feelings of betrayal or abandonment if these figures fail to meet those expectations.

For instance, consider Alex, who turned to her uncle as a father substitute. She idolized him, viewing him as the paternal figure she had been missing. Initially, he provided the affection and support she craved, but as Alex grew older, she began to see him as flawed, struggling to reconcile her idealized image of him with reality. This disillusionment prompted a crisis of self-worth; Alex felt abandoned again, reflecting her deep-rooted fears of unworthiness and rejection.

Moreover, the search for validation can lead to unhealthy patterns of dependency. A daughter may feel compelled to cater to the needs of male figures in her life, prioritizing their approval over her own well-being. This dynamic can create a cycle of emotional instability, where her sense of self is heavily reliant on external validation, making it difficult for her to cultivate an independent identity.

The Role of Peers and Media

The search for approval is not confined to family relationships; it often extends to peer groups and media influences. As daughters navigate adolescence, the desire for male validation can manifest in their interactions with friends and romantic interests. The pressure to conform to societal standards of beauty and behavior can amplify this search for approval, leading daughters to prioritize relationships with males who reinforce these ideals.

The media plays a significant role in shaping these perceptions. The portrayal of relationships in movies, television shows, and social media can create unrealistic expectations, prompting daughters to equate their self-worth with male attention and approval. Social media platforms, in particular, can exacerbate feelings of inadequacy, as daughters compare themselves to curated images of others who seemingly receive abundant validation from male figures.

Consider the example of Zoe, who became heavily invested in social media as a means of connecting with others. She found herself obsessively seeking likes and comments from male followers, believing that their attention would validate her worth. The fleeting nature of social media interactions, however, only deepened her feelings of inadequacy when the approval she craved didn't materialize. This cycle of seeking validation through external sources further eroded her sense of self, leaving her feeling empty and unfulfilled.

The Impact on Self-Identity

The pursuit of approval from male figures can profoundly impact a daughter's self-identity. Without a father's guidance, she may struggle to form a solid sense of self, relying heavily on external validation to define her worth. This dependence can hinder her ability to make autonomous decisions, as she constantly weighs her choices against the potential approval or disapproval of others.

As daughters navigate their search for validation, they may find themselves caught in a cycle of self-doubt and insecurity. The constant need for affirmation can lead to an identity that is fragmented and reactive, rather than authentic and self-driven. This struggle can result in a lack of confidence in their abilities, making it difficult for them to pursue goals and dreams independent of others' opinions.

The Path Toward Healing

Recognizing the impact of seeking validation from male figures is essential for daughters as they navigate their emotional journeys. Building self-esteem from within rather than relying solely on external sources is crucial for developing a strong and positive self-identity. Engaging in activities that promote self-discovery, such as journaling, therapy, or creative expression, can help daughters cultivate a deeper understanding of their worth independent of others' approval.

Encouraging healthy relationships with male figures, where mutual respect and support exist, can also aid in the healing process. By setting boundaries and fostering connections based on authentic respect rather than dependency, daughters can begin to redefine their relationships with men and understand their value beyond the quest for validation.

Empowerment Through Self-Validation

The search for approval and validation from other male figures is a common emotional response among daughters who have experienced father absence. This quest can shape their relationships, self-esteem, and overall identity. However, it is essential to recognize that true validation must come from within.

Through self-reflection, awareness, and healthy relationship-building, daughters can learn to validate themselves, fostering resilience and independence. By understanding their inherent worth, they can break free from the cycle of seeking approval and instead embrace a journey of self-discovery and empowerment. As they navigate the complexities of their emotional landscape, daughters can emerge with a renewed sense of self, one that celebrates their uniqueness and fosters authentic connections with others.

Chapter 4:

Behavioral and Social Effects

A. How Father Absence Affects Daughters' Behaviors - Rebellion, Attention-Seeking, and Withdrawal

The absence of a father can significantly influence a daughter's behavior and social interactions. It can lead to a range of emotional responses that manifest in rebellion, attention-seeking behaviors, and withdrawal. Understanding these behavioral patterns is crucial in comprehending the broader impact of father absence on a daughter's psychological and social development.

The Roots of Rebellion

Rebellion is one of the most observable behavioral effects in daughters who grow up without a father. This rebellion can take various forms, including defiance of authority, participation in risky behaviors, and an overall disregard for rules. At its core, rebellion often stems from deep emotional pain and unresolved feelings regarding abandonment.

Consider the story of Lily, a bright teenager who began engaging in increasingly risky behaviors as she navigated her formative years without her father. Lily's rebellious actions - skipping school, experimenting with substances, and openly defying her mother - were not merely acts of defiance; they were expressions of her inner turmoil. Each rebellious act was a cry for help, a way for her to seek control in a life that felt chaotic due to her father's absence. Lily felt that by pushing boundaries, she was asserting her independence. However, this behavior also alienated her from her peers and family, creating a cycle of isolation that further fueled her rebellion.

Psychologists suggest that this kind of behavior is often linked to a daughter's search for identity and belonging. In the absence of a father figure, daughters may struggle to understand their place in the world. Rebellion becomes a way to carve out an identity, albeit a tumultuous one. As daughters act out against societal norms or family expectations, they may find a sense of power in their rebellion, compensating for the lack of paternal guidance and support.

Attention-Seeking Behaviors

In contrast to outright rebellion, some daughters respond to their father's absence with attention-seeking behaviors. This pattern often emerges from a desperate need for validation and connection, resulting in actions aimed at drawing attention from peers, teachers, or other authority figures. Daughters who feel neglected may engage in both positive and negative attention-seeking behaviors, from excelling in school to acting out disruptively in class.

Take the case of Sarah, who, in her early years, became a model student, often going above and beyond to impress her teachers and earn their praise. However, as she transitioned into adolescence, her behaviors shifted dramatically. The lack of a father in her life created an emotional void that she tried to fill by becoming the class clown, engaging in outlandish antics to garner laughter and attention. Sarah's shift highlighted the dual nature of attention-seeking; while she initially sought validation through academic achievement, she ultimately resorted to disruptive behavior when she felt that her efforts were unnoticed.

This need for attention can often manifest as an insatiable craving for affirmation from male peers or figures, complicating relationships with both friends and authority. For instance, daughters may flirt with male classmates or teachers, believing that gaining attention from them could help fill the void left by their absent fathers. However, this can lead to misunderstandings and unhealthy dynamics, where the daughter feels valued only for her appearance or charm rather than her character or intellect.

Withdrawal and Emotional Isolation

On the other end of the spectrum, some daughters respond to their father's absence with withdrawal and emotional isolation. Rather than acting out or seeking attention, these daughters may retreat into themselves, developing an internal world that becomes a refuge from the pain of abandonment. This behavior is often rooted in feelings of shame, unworthiness, or confusion regarding their identity.

Emma's story illustrates this well. After her father left, she gradually became more introverted, distancing herself from friends and family. The absence of her father left her grappling with feelings of rejection, leading her to believe that she was unlovable. In social settings, she often felt like an outsider, withdrawing from conversations and avoiding interactions. Emma's withdrawal was a defense mechanism; by isolating herself, she attempted to protect her heart from further pain and disappointment. However, this behavior only perpetuated her feelings of loneliness, creating a cycle that was difficult to break.

Psychologically, withdrawal can be a protective response to trauma. Daughters who experience the absence of a father may feel they cannot trust others, leading to a pervasive sense of isolation. This lack of social engagement can hinder their development of essential social skills, making it challenging to form meaningful relationships later in life. As these daughters navigate their emotional struggles in solitude, they may miss out on valuable opportunities for connection, support, and healing.

The Interconnectedness of Behaviors

It is important to note that rebellion, attention-seeking, and withdrawal are not mutually exclusive; many daughters exhibit a combination of these behaviors as they navigate the complexities of their emotions. The absence of a father creates a unique emotional landscape, one that can foster a wide range of responses. For instance, a daughter may act out rebelliously in one situation but withdraw in another, depending on her emotional state and the specific context she finds herself in.

Understanding these behavioral patterns requires a nuanced approach. Daughters' responses to father absence are often informed by their personalities, their family dynamics, and their social environments. For instance, daughters with strong support systems may be less likely to engage in rebellious behavior or withdrawal, as they have other sources of validation and connection. Conversely, those who lack supportive relationships may find themselves trapped in cycles of acting out or retreating into emotional isolation.

The Role of Support Systems

Creating a supportive environment is crucial for helping daughters navigate the challenges posed by father absence. This support can come from various sources - mothers, extended family, mentors, or friends. A nurturing support system can help mitigate the negative behavioral impacts associated with father absence by providing emotional stability and affirmation.

In the case of Mia, who struggled with rebellion, her mother's efforts to communicate openly about her father's absence and provide consistent love and support became pivotal. With her mother's guidance, Mia learned to channel her rebellious energy into more constructive outlets, such as sports and creative endeavors. This support not only helped Mia find healthier ways to express her emotions but also fostered a sense of identity that was less dependent on her father's presence.

Navigating the Effects of Father Absence

The behavioral and social effects of father absence are complex and multifaceted, encompassing a range of responses including rebellion, attention-seeking, and withdrawal. These behaviors reflect the underlying emotional struggles faced by daughters who grapple with feelings of abandonment and the search for identity in the absence of paternal support.

Recognizing and understanding these behaviors is essential for fostering healthier emotional development in daughters affected by father absence. Through supportive relationships, open communication, and self-discovery, daughters can navigate their emotional landscapes more effectively, ultimately leading to a stronger sense of self and healthier social interactions. By addressing these challenges, we can empower daughters to redefine their identities and forge meaningful connections, transforming the impact of father absence into opportunities for growth and resilience.

B. Struggles with Authority and Male Figures in Society

The absence of a father during childhood can lead to significant struggles in a daughter's relationship with authority figures, particularly male ones. This dynamic plays a crucial role in shaping her social interactions, self-image, and overall emotional development. Understanding these struggles requires an exploration of the psychological implications of father absence and the ways it can lead to challenges in navigating authority and forming healthy relationships with male figures.

The Psychological Impact of Father Absence

Father absence often leaves a profound void in a daughter's emotional landscape, which can lead to feelings of insecurity and confusion regarding male figures in her life. The father typically embodies a figure of authority, protection, and guidance. Without this presence, daughters may struggle to develop a sense of security and trust in authority, leading to apprehensions about engaging with male figures later in life.

For instance, Jessica, a bright young woman, found herself constantly clashing with her male teachers in school. Her father had left when she was very young, and she grew up feeling a sense of betrayal and anger towards men. Whenever a male authority figure addressed her, she felt an instinctive urge to rebel, viewing their guidance as a threat rather than support. This instinctive rebellion was less about the authority figure's actions and more about her unresolved feelings about her father's absence. The root of Jessica's struggles lay in her emotional response to male authority; she could not differentiate between constructive criticism and the feelings of abandonment she associated with her father's departure.

The Fear of Abandonment and Authority

The fear of abandonment, often prevalent in daughters of absent fathers, can also exacerbate struggles with authority. Daughters may develop a deep-seated anxiety regarding male figures, perceiving them as potential sources of pain or disappointment. This perception can manifest as hostility, resentment, or outright defiance in response to authority.

Consider Mia, who often found herself in heated arguments with male authority figures, whether they were teachers, coaches, or family friends. Her father's absence had instilled a belief that men were unreliable, and this belief colored her interactions with them. Whenever a male figure attempted to enforce rules or provide guidance, Mia's first instinct was to push back aggressively. She feared that by submitting to authority, she would be vulnerable to emotional pain - just as she had felt with her father. Mia's defiance was not merely a challenge to authority; it was a defense mechanism designed to shield her from the potential for emotional hurt.

The Quest for Male Validation

In the absence of a father, daughters often seek validation from male figures in their lives, leading to complex dynamics that can further complicate their relationship with authority. This quest for validation can result in daughters being overly accommodating or excessively deferential to male authority figures, which can create a dangerous cycle of dependency.

Take the example of Sophie, a high-achieving student who consistently sought approval from her male teachers. While her dedication to her studies was admirable, her need for validation often translated into an inability to assert herself in the classroom. Sophie frequently allowed her male peers to dominate discussions, believing that by staying quiet, she would earn their respect. However, this approach left her feeling invisible and undervalued, ultimately leading to frustration and resentment toward her male classmates. Her struggle stemmed from a desire to fill the emotional void left by her absent father, leading her to equate male attention with worthiness.

The Role of Authority Figures

The relationship with authority figures, particularly male ones, becomes a complex tapestry woven with threads of past experiences, emotional needs, and societal expectations. In this context, male authority figures can inadvertently reinforce the feelings of inadequacy and mistrust that daughters of absent fathers experience. When these figures act with authority, it may unintentionally trigger memories of their father's absence, leading to defensive behaviors that undermine constructive interactions.

Consider the story of Claire, a young woman who faced ongoing challenges in her workplace with her male supervisor. Despite being a competent employee, Claire often found herself feeling undermined and overlooked in meetings. Whenever her supervisor would challenge her ideas or provide feedback, she would react defensively, interpreting his feedback as criticism rather than guidance. Claire's emotional responses were deeply rooted in her experiences with her father; she viewed male authority as a threat to her self-worth.

This dynamic highlights the need for sensitivity and understanding from authority figures when dealing with daughters of absent fathers. Effective male mentors or leaders can play a crucial role in counteracting negative experiences by providing consistent support and validation. When male authority figures adopt a compassionate and encouraging approach, they can help daughters navigate their emotional struggles and build healthier relationships with authority.

Building Trust and Resilience

To overcome the challenges associated with father absence, daughters must learn to build trust in authority figures and develop resilience in their social interactions. This process often involves confronting and reframing negative beliefs about male authority.

Engagement with supportive male figures - such as mentors, coaches, or teachers - can provide a foundation for rebuilding trust. These positive experiences can help daughters redefine their perceptions of authority, transforming fear and mistrust into respect and collaboration. The key is for daughters to encounter consistent, nurturing, and affirming interactions with male figures who embody supportive authority.

An example of this can be seen in Emily, a young girl who initially struggled with her male teachers due to her father's absence. However, through her participation in a mentorship program, she connected with a compassionate male mentor who encouraged her strengths and listened to her concerns. As a result, Emily gradually began to reframe her understanding of male authority. Instead of viewing it as a source of threat, she started to see it as an opportunity for guidance and growth. This transformation marked a turning point in her life, enabling her to engage more positively with authority figures in various aspects of her life.

Navigating Authority in a Fatherless Landscape

The struggles with authority and male figures in society that daughters of absent fathers face are profound and complex. These struggles can manifest as rebellion, anxiety, or a quest for validation, often rooted in the emotional challenges of navigating a fatherless upbringing.

However, through intentional engagement with supportive male figures and a commitment to building trust, daughters can learn to navigate these challenges effectively. By fostering resilience and reframing their experiences, they can ultimately cultivate healthier relationships with authority and discover their worth beyond the shadows of their fathers' absence. As they embark on this journey, they can transform their past struggles into empowering narratives that lead to personal growth and emotional healing, creating a brighter future filled with confidence and self-acceptance.

C. Impact on Peer Relationships and Social Interactions

The absence of a father during childhood profoundly influences a daughter's peer relationships and social interactions. This impact often manifests in various ways, affecting not only how daughters relate to their peers but also their ability to navigate social settings, establish meaningful friendships, and develop essential social skills. Understanding these dynamics is crucial for recognizing the long-term effects of father absence on emotional and psychological development.

Emotional Responses and Peer Interactions

Daughters raised without a father may experience heightened emotional responses in social situations. This absence can lead to feelings of insecurity, loneliness, and vulnerability, which often hinder the formation of healthy relationships. When peers sense this emotional fragility, it can create barriers to connection, leading to misunderstandings and a cycle of social withdrawal.

For instance, consider Lily, a young girl who grew up without her father. At school, she often found herself on the fringes of social groups, struggling to initiate conversations or join activities. Her classmates, sensing her hesitation, sometimes interpreted her quietness as aloofness or unfriendliness, which further isolated her. Lily's emotional responses - rooted in her father's absence - made it difficult for her to approach others with confidence, leading to missed opportunities for friendship and support. In this way, the lack of a father figure not only affected her self-esteem but also her ability to engage socially.

Trust Issues and Vulnerability

The absence of a father can also lead to significant trust issues in peer relationships. Daughters may develop a defensive stance, fearing betrayal or rejection from their peers, which can hinder their ability to form deep and meaningful connections. This protective behavior is often a response to the emotional neglect associated with father absence, creating a barrier to intimacy in friendships.

Take the example of Emma, who, despite her friendly demeanor, struggled to trust her friends. Having been abandoned by her father, she frequently worried that her friends would also leave her. As a result, Emma often kept them at arm's length, avoiding discussions about her feelings or personal life. This lack of vulnerability limited her ability to connect with others authentically, resulting in superficial relationships that left her feeling unfulfilled. Her experiences illustrate how the emotional scars of father absence can influence trust and connection in peer interactions.

Social Skills Development

Social skills are essential for navigating the complexities of relationships, and father absence can impede the development of these critical abilities. Fathers often play a vital role in teaching their daughters how to interact with others, model appropriate behavior, and manage conflicts. Without this guidance, daughters may struggle with social cues, conflict resolution, and communication skills.

For instance, Sarah, a bright but socially awkward young girl, often found herself in challenging situations with her peers. Lacking a father figure to guide her through social nuances, she would often misinterpret jokes or fail to recognize when her friends were upset. Her awkwardness resulted in frequent misunderstandings, causing her to feel frustrated and alienated. This difficulty in navigating social interactions stemmed from her inability to learn from a male role model, ultimately affecting her confidence and enjoyment in social settings.

Peer Pressure and Risky Behavior

Daughters without an engaged father figure may also be more susceptible to peer pressure, particularly in adolescence. The absence of a father can lead to a yearning for validation from peers, which may result in a greater willingness to engage in risky or harmful behaviors to fit in or gain acceptance.

Take the case of Jenna, a teenager who, feeling isolated from her peers, sought out friendships with a group known for their rebellious activities. Her need for acceptance led her to participate in risky behaviors, such as skipping school and experimenting with substances. Jenna's actions were driven by a desire to find belonging, stemming from the void left by her father's absence. In this scenario, the lack of a father figure contributed to her susceptibility to negative influences, ultimately jeopardizing her well-being.

The Role of Alternative Support Systems

While the absence of a father can create significant challenges, many daughters find solace in alternative support systems. Mentors, teachers, and even positive relationships with male family members can provide the guidance and support necessary for healthy social development. These figures can help fill the void left by an absent father, teaching essential social skills and fostering emotional resilience.

For example, Mia, who grew up without her father, formed a close bond with her high school guidance counselor, a compassionate and understanding man. Through their interactions, Mia learned valuable lessons about trust, communication, and self-acceptance. Her counselor encouraged her to engage with her peers more openly, helping her navigate social situations with greater confidence. This positive mentorship became a pivotal factor in Mia's social development, demonstrating the importance of supportive figures in the absence of a father.

Building Positive Relationships

Ultimately, while the absence of a father can significantly impact a daughter's peer relationships and social interactions, it is essential to recognize that healing and growth are possible. By fostering emotional intelligence, encouraging open communication, and providing opportunities for positive social experiences, daughters can learn to navigate the complexities of relationships successfully.

Support from family, friends, and mentors can facilitate the development of crucial social skills, enabling daughters to build meaningful connections and foster healthy relationships. As they learn to trust and engage with others, they can create a sense of community and belonging that mitigates the effects of father absence.

The Journey Towards Connection

The impact of father absence on peer relationships and social interactions is profound, influencing emotional responses, trust, social skills development, and susceptibility to peer pressure. Daughters may experience challenges in forming healthy relationships, navigating social situations, and developing the necessary skills to thrive in their social environments.

However, with the right support and opportunities, daughters can transform their experiences into strengths, fostering resilience and emotional intelligence. By addressing the effects of father absence and cultivating positive relationships, they can embark on a journey toward connection, belonging, and personal growth. In doing so, they can overcome the challenges associated with their upbringing and forge a brighter future filled with fulfilling relationships and self-acceptance.

Chapter 5:

Academic and Cognitive Effects

A. Lower Academic Achievement

The absence of a father during childhood can significantly impede a daughter's academic performance. Research consistently shows that children raised in father-absent homes often experience lower grades and reduced educational attainment compared to their peers from intact families. This disparity is frequently attributed to several interrelated factors, including emotional distress, lack of motivation, and insufficient support structures.

Without the guiding presence of a father, many daughters struggle to find the encouragement and reinforcement needed to excel academically. For instance, consider a young girl named Sophie, who, growing up in a single-parent household, often felt overwhelmed by her schoolwork. The absence of her father not only left a void in her emotional support system but also resulted in fewer resources available at home to assist with her studies. As her mother juggled multiple jobs, the time for homework assistance diminished. Consequently, Sophie's grades began to slip, and her ambition waned as she began to internalize the belief that academic success was beyond her reach. This cycle illustrates how the lack of a father figure can contribute to lower academic achievement, perpetuating feelings of inadequacy and despair.

Difficulty Concentrating

Daughters raised in father-absent households often face challenges with concentration and focus in their academic pursuits. The emotional turmoil stemming from father absence can lead to heightened levels of anxiety, depression, and insecurity, all of which can detract from a child's ability to concentrate on their studies. The mental energy that could be directed toward learning is frequently diverted to managing feelings of abandonment or seeking affirmation from peers.

For example, Emma, a bright student, often found herself daydreaming during class, her thoughts drifting to memories of her father who had left when she was just a toddler. Despite her intelligence, she struggled to pay attention, her mind clouded by feelings of loss and confusion. This distraction impacted her grades and participation in class, leading her teachers to believe she lacked interest or motivation. However, the reality was much more complex; Emma was battling a silent struggle that diminished her ability to concentrate on her studies. Her experience underscores the profound cognitive effects that father absence can have on a daughter's academic engagement and focus.

Reduced Ambition

The absence of a father figure can also lead to a significant reduction in ambition and drive among daughters. Fathers often serve as role models, inspiring their daughters to pursue their goals and dreams. When this guidance is absent, young girls may find it challenging to envision a future filled with possibilities, leading to diminished aspirations and an inability to set and achieve academic goals.

Take the case of Mia, who, after her father left, lost her sense of direction and motivation. Once a girl with dreams of becoming a veterinarian, she began to see her ambitions fade as her home life became chaotic. The emotional burden of her father's absence loomed large, overshadowing her dreams. Without the encouragement to pursue her aspirations, Mia settled for mediocrity, believing that her goals were unattainable. Her story exemplifies how the lack of a father figure can extinguish a young girl's ambition, leaving her adrift in a sea of uncertainty.

The Role of Emotional Support

The importance of emotional support in academic achievement cannot be overstated. Fathers often play a critical role in providing the encouragement and motivation necessary for academic success. Without this support, daughters may struggle to cultivate resilience, discipline, and a sense of self-worth - qualities that are integral to overcoming academic challenges.

In the case of Sophie, the emotional distance from her father translated into a lack of confidence in her abilities. With limited support at home, she began to doubt her potential, leading to a vicious cycle of underachievement. As she faced academic difficulties, her self-esteem plummeted, reinforcing the belief that she would never succeed. This downward spiral illustrates how the absence of a father can profoundly impact a daughter's emotional health, ultimately hindering her academic progress.

Academic Support Structures

While the absence of a father can create significant obstacles, it is essential to recognize that alternative support structures can mitigate these effects. Positive relationships with teachers, mentors, and other family members can help fill the void left by an absent father, providing the encouragement and resources needed for academic success.

For instance, Mia found an unexpected ally in her high school biology teacher, who recognized her potential and took the time to mentor her. Through this relationship, Mia regained her passion for science and developed the confidence to pursue her goal of veterinary medicine. The support from her teacher played a pivotal role in her academic journey, highlighting the importance of cultivating positive relationships in the absence of a father.

Building Resilience

Ultimately, the effects of father absence on academic achievement, concentration, and ambition are profound, but they are not insurmountable. By fostering resilience, encouraging open communication, and providing opportunities for growth, daughters can overcome the challenges associated with father absence.

Support from family, friends, and mentors can create a nurturing environment that encourages academic engagement and emotional well-being. By addressing the underlying emotional issues and cultivating a sense of belonging, daughters can develop the skills and confidence needed to navigate the complexities of academic life.

A Path Forward

The effects of father absence on academic and cognitive development are multifaceted, encompassing lower academic achievement, difficulty concentrating, and reduced ambition. While the absence of a father can create significant challenges, it is essential to recognize the potential for healing and growth. Through supportive relationships, emotional resilience, and a commitment to education, daughters can overcome the obstacles posed by father absence and strive toward a future filled with possibilities. As they embark on this journey, they can transform their experiences into strengths, ultimately finding their voices and pursuing their dreams with renewed determination.

B. Correlation Between Father Absence and School Drop-Out Rates

The impact of father absence on a child's academic trajectory is profound, with a significant correlation between father absence and school drop-out rates. Numerous studies have established that children raised in father-absent households are statistically more likely to leave school before completing their education. This trend can be attributed to various factors, including emotional distress, a lack of support and guidance, and socioeconomic challenges.

Emotional Distress and Motivation

When a father is absent, the emotional distress that often ensues can lead to decreased motivation among daughters. The absence of a father figure can create feelings of abandonment and insecurity, which can manifest in a lack of enthusiasm for school. For instance, consider a girl named Lily, who faced the dual challenge of navigating adolescence while dealing with the emotional fallout of her father's departure. The emotional burden of his absence weighed heavily on her, affecting her ability to focus on her studies. Instead of engaging with her education, Lily found herself increasingly disinterested, viewing school as a reminder of her fractured family. This emotional disconnect ultimately contributed to her decision to drop out, illustrating how father absence can erode motivation and lead to a disengagement from academic responsibilities.

Lack of Guidance and Support

The absence of a father often results in a lack of guidance and support that is crucial during the formative years of education. Fathers typically play a pivotal role in shaping their children's aspirations, offering encouragement and setting expectations. Without this guiding presence, many daughters may struggle to find the direction necessary to navigate their educational journeys effectively.

Take, for example, Sarah, a bright and talented student who once excelled in her studies. After her father left, the dynamics at home shifted dramatically. Her mother, overwhelmed by the responsibilities of being a single parent, could not provide the same level of academic support that Sarah once received. As a result, Sarah began to feel lost and unsupported, lacking the encouragement needed to push through challenges. With no one to help her set academic goals or provide guidance, she gradually lost interest in her education and eventually decided to drop out of school, seeking solace in other areas of life.

Socioeconomic Challenges

Father absence often correlates with increased socioeconomic challenges, which can further exacerbate the risk of dropping out of school. Single-parent households typically face financial difficulties, leading to limited resources for educational support. This lack of financial stability can result in inadequate access to academic resources, such as tutoring or extracurricular activities, that could otherwise bolster a child's educational experience.

For instance, in many cases, daughters from father-absent households may have to take on responsibilities at home, such as caring for younger siblings or contributing to household income, which can detract from their academic pursuits. A girl named Emily, for example, had to forego her studies to work part-time after her father left, diminishing her academic performance and increasing her likelihood of dropping out. The harsh reality is that when children must prioritize immediate financial needs over education, the long-term consequences can be detrimental, perpetuating cycles of poverty and educational disadvantage.

Poor Academic Performance

The correlation between father absence and poor academic performance is a significant area of concern. Studies indicate that children from father-absent homes consistently achieve lower academic outcomes compared to their peers. The psychological effects of father absence can manifest in difficulties with concentration, lower self-esteem, and a lack of engagement in school activities, all of which contribute to poor academic performance.

For instance, Jessica was once a straight-A student, but following her father's departure, her grades began to plummet. The emotional turmoil she experienced made it difficult for her to concentrate on her schoolwork. As she grappled with feelings of sadness and anxiety, her once-bright academic prospects dimmed. Teachers noticed her disengagement and offered support, but Jessica felt isolated and overwhelmed. Her grades suffered, demonstrating how the absence of a father can lead to a decline in academic performance and a sense of hopelessness about future prospects.

Long-Term Consequences

The long-term consequences of father absence on academic achievement extend beyond immediate performance issues. Poor academic outcomes often have cascading effects, limiting opportunities for higher education and career advancement. Daughters who drop out of school or perform poorly academically may find themselves trapped in low-paying jobs, struggling to provide for themselves and their families, thus perpetuating a cycle of disadvantage.

Consider the story of Mia, who dropped out of high school due to the emotional burden of her father's absence. As she entered adulthood, her lack of education restricted her career options, leading to a series of low-wage jobs that barely covered her living expenses. The absence of a father not only robbed her of educational opportunities but also hindered her ability to break free from the socioeconomic challenges that plagued her family. Mia's journey exemplifies how the effects of father absence can reverberate through generations, shaping not only individual lives but also the broader fabric of society.

Addressing the Impact of Father Absence

The correlation between father absence and school drop-out rates and poor academic performance is clear and concerning. The emotional, social, and economic ramifications of growing up without a father can significantly impair a daughter's educational experience, leading to disengagement from school and diminished aspirations. However, it is crucial to recognize that while father absence presents formidable challenges, intervention and support systems can help mitigate these effects.

Encouraging mentorship programs, providing resources for single-parent households, and fostering positive educational environments can help bridge the gap left by absent fathers. By prioritizing emotional support and academic encouragement, society can empower daughters to overcome the obstacles posed by father absence and strive toward a future filled with educational opportunities and success.

Chapter 6:

Relationship Challenges

A. How Absent Fathers Influence Romantic Relationships

The impact of a father's absence extends far beyond childhood, permeating the fabric of an adult daughter's romantic relationships. Research indicates that daughters who grow up without an involved father often carry the emotional and psychological scars of that absence into their adult lives. These scars manifest in various ways, shaping their perceptions of love, intimacy, and trust. Understanding these dynamics is essential for grasping the complexity of relationships formed under the shadow of father absence.

Emotional Attachment Styles

One of the most significant influences of father absence on adult daughters is the development of emotional attachment styles. According to attachment theory, early interactions with primary caregivers form the blueprint for how individuals approach relationships in adulthood. Daughters who experience father absence may develop insecure attachment styles, characterized by anxiety, avoidance, or ambivalence.

For instance, consider the story of Maya, who grew up with a father who left when she was just a toddler. As she entered her teenage years and began to explore romantic relationships, Maya found herself oscillating between clinging to her partners out of fear of abandonment and pushing them away to protect herself from potential heartbreak. This push-pull dynamic created confusion and tension in her relationships, often leading to the very outcomes she feared: rejection and abandonment. Her struggles exemplify how father absence can give rise to attachment issues that complicate the pursuit of healthy, stable romantic relationships.

Trust Issues

Daughters raised in father-absent households often grapple with profound trust issues. The absence of a father figure can lead to a pervasive fear of betrayal or abandonment, making it challenging for these daughters to open themselves up fully to their partners. For instance, Sarah, who navigated her adult relationships with trepidation, constantly second-guessed her partners' intentions. Her father's abandonment had ingrained in her a belief that love was conditional and that her partners might leave her at any moment.

This distrust manifested as a defensive mechanism; she often found herself scrutinizing her partners' every move, interpreting innocent actions as signs of infidelity or emotional distance. Consequently, her relationships became fraught with conflict, as her need for reassurance clashed with her partner's attempts to provide support. This cycle of mistrust ultimately hindered Sarah's ability to cultivate healthy, fulfilling relationships, leaving her feeling isolated and disillusioned.

The Search for Validation

A father's absence can also lead to a heightened need for validation from romantic partners. Daughters may unconsciously seek out relationships that can fill the emotional void left by their fathers, leading them to idealize their partners in unhealthy ways. For example, Jasmine, who grew up without her father, often found herself in relationships with men who displayed dominant or controlling behaviors. The desire for affirmation led her to tolerate mistreatment, as she equated attention with love.

In her quest for validation, Jasmine often ignored red flags and rationalized unhealthy behaviors, believing that any attention, even if negative, was better than the emptiness she felt from her father's absence. This pattern not only left her vulnerable to emotionally abusive relationships but also perpetuated her feelings of worthlessness. The connection between absent fathers and the need for validation illuminates a poignant aspect of how father absence can distort an adult daughter's perception of love and self-worth.

Fear of Intimacy

Interestingly, father absence can result in a paradoxical fear of intimacy. While some daughters crave closeness, the emotional wounds from their father's absence may trigger anxiety when faced with genuine intimacy. Take the case of Emily, who, after years of yearning for a loving relationship, found herself pulling away whenever her partner expressed feelings of affection. The prospect of being truly vulnerable terrified her, as it echoed the vulnerability she felt as a child when her father left.

This fear of intimacy often leads to an emotional distance that can sabotage relationships. For Emily, her partner's expressions of love were met with apprehension, and instead of reciprocating affection, she would retreat into herself. The cycle of longing for connection while simultaneously fearing it underscores the complexity of emotional responses that daughters of absent fathers experience in their romantic lives.

Repeating Patterns

The patterns established during childhood can lead to a cycle of repeating relational dynamics in adulthood. Daughters may unconsciously gravitate toward partners who mirror the emotional unavailability they experienced with their fathers. This tendency can perpetuate a cycle of heartbreak and disappointment. For instance, when Rachel began dating, she found herself drawn to men who exhibited similar traits to her father - those who were charismatic yet emotionally distant.

Rachel's inability to recognize the pattern meant she often entered relationships filled with hope, only to find herself facing familiar disappointments. Her relationships echoed the emotional landscape of her childhood, leaving her feeling trapped in a cycle that she desperately wished to escape. Recognizing these patterns is vital for healing and breaking free from the shadows of the past.

Healing and Growth

The influence of absent fathers on adult daughters' romantic relationships is a multifaceted issue, rooted in emotional attachment styles, trust issues, and the search for validation. However, understanding these dynamics is the first step toward healing and growth. Through therapy, support networks, and self-reflection, daughters can learn to identify and confront the patterns that hinder their romantic lives.

Moreover, fostering a sense of self-worth and developing healthy communication skills are crucial in reshaping relationship dynamics. While the impact of a father's absence is significant, it is not insurmountable. Many daughters find ways to redefine their relationships, drawing strength from their experiences and striving for healthier, more fulfilling connections. By addressing the emotional legacies left by absent fathers, adult daughters can pave the way for a future filled with love, intimacy, and resilience.

B. Trust Issues, Attachment Styles, and Difficulty in Sustaining Healthy Relationships

The absence of a father figure during formative years can create a ripple effect that influences many aspects of an adult daughter's life, particularly in her romantic relationships. Trust issues and attachment styles developed in response to this absence can severely complicate the formation and maintenance of healthy relationships. As daughters navigate their adult lives, they often find themselves entangled in complex emotional patterns that hinder their ability to connect with others. Understanding these dynamics is crucial for both daughters and those seeking to support them.

Trust Issues: The Shadows of Abandonment

One of the most profound impacts of father absence is the development of trust issues. Trust is a fundamental component of any healthy relationship, yet for daughters who have experienced the abandonment of a father, establishing trust can feel like an insurmountable challenge. The psychological scars left by a father's absence often breed a deep-seated fear of betrayal, which can manifest as paranoia or excessive suspicion in future relationships.

For example, consider Mia, who was abandoned by her father at a young age. As an adult, Mia found herself in relationships marked by her inability to trust her partners fully. Each time her partner received a text message, Mia's heart raced with anxiety, convinced that there was someone more important in his life. This persistent distrust created a toxic environment that ultimately led to the downfall of her relationships. The underlying belief that no one could be trusted made it difficult for Mia to build meaningful connections, leaving her isolated and feeling unworthy of love.

Attachment Styles: The Blueprint of Relationships

The way individuals attach to others in relationships is often shaped by early experiences with primary caregivers. According to attachment theory, there are four primary attachment styles: secure, anxious, avoidant, and disorganized. Daughters raised in father-absent households frequently develop insecure attachment styles, particularly anxious or avoidant patterns, which can dictate how they interact with romantic partners.

For instance, Lisa, whose father left when she was very young, developed an anxious attachment style. As an adult, she found herself obsessively seeking reassurance from her partners. Each time they failed to respond to a text quickly or showed signs of emotional distance, Lisa spiraled into a state of panic. Her constant need for validation created a heavy emotional burden on her partners, who often felt overwhelmed and frustrated. This pattern not only strained her relationships but also left Lisa feeling unfulfilled and disconnected, perpetuating a cycle of anxiety and insecurity.

On the other hand, some daughters may develop avoidant attachment styles, characterized by emotional distance and reluctance to fully engage in relationships. Julia, who had a father who was physically present but emotionally unavailable, often found herself pushing partners away whenever they attempted to get too close. This behavior stemmed from her fear of vulnerability, as opening up felt akin to exposing herself to the same disappointment she had experienced in her childhood. Julia's struggles illustrate how attachment styles shaped by father absence can create barriers to emotional intimacy and trust, making it challenging for her to sustain healthy relationships.

Difficulty Sustaining Healthy Relationships

As a result of trust issues and maladaptive attachment styles, many daughters of absent fathers struggle to sustain healthy, long-term relationships. The cycle of mistrust, anxiety, and emotional distance creates a fertile ground for conflict and misunderstanding, often leading to relationship breakdowns. The emotional scars from childhood can resurface during times of stress or conflict, causing daughters to react in ways that sabotage their connections.

Take the story of Hannah, who entered adulthood with a deep yearning for connection but was plagued by a fear of abandonment. Each time her partner expressed frustration or needed space, Hannah interpreted it as a sign of impending rejection. In a bid to regain control, she would react defensively, often escalating minor disagreements into significant conflicts. Her inability to navigate these emotional storms left her partners feeling exasperated and confused, ultimately contributing to the dissolution of her relationships.

This pattern is not unique to Hannah. Many daughters who grew up without a father figure may find themselves trapped in a cycle of seeking love while simultaneously pushing it away. The internal conflict between the desire for intimacy and the fear of vulnerability creates a paradox that complicates their romantic lives. As these daughters navigate relationships, the emotional baggage they carry can impede their ability to communicate effectively, leading to misunderstandings and unmet needs.

The Path Toward Healing

Despite the challenges posed by trust issues and attachment styles, healing is possible. Recognizing these patterns and understanding their origins is the first step toward breaking the cycle of dysfunction. Therapy can provide a safe space for daughters to explore their feelings, confront their fears, and develop healthier coping mechanisms.

Additionally, open and honest communication with partners can foster understanding and support. For instance, when Mia began to acknowledge her trust issues and communicated her fears to her partner, they were able to work together to build a foundation of trust. This process required patience and vulnerability, but it ultimately strengthened their relationship.

Moreover, engaging in self-reflection can empower daughters to redefine their relationship with love and intimacy. By recognizing the patterns that have emerged as a result of their father's absence, they can actively choose to challenge those narratives and seek healthier relationships.

Reclaiming the Narrative

The long-term consequences of father absence are profound, affecting adult daughters in multifaceted ways that complicate their romantic relationships. Trust issues, maladaptive attachment styles, and difficulties sustaining healthy connections can create a complex web of emotional struggles. However, through self-awareness, therapy, and open communication, daughters can begin to reclaim their narratives.

Ultimately, understanding the impact of a father's absence is not merely about acknowledging the pain; it is about empowering daughters to break free from the shadows of their past. By fostering healthier relationships, daughters can rewrite their stories, paving the way for connections built on trust, intimacy, and genuine love. The journey toward healing may be challenging, but it holds the promise of transforming relationships into sources of strength and fulfillment.

C. Patterns of Dating Emotionally Unavailable Partners

For many adult daughters who grew up without a father figure, the patterns of emotional connection - or disconnection - can significantly shape their romantic relationships. A common phenomenon among these daughters is the tendency to gravitate toward emotionally unavailable partners. This inclination is often rooted in unresolved childhood traumas and reflects a complex interplay of desire and fear that ultimately shapes their dating choices. Understanding why this pattern emerges and its implications is vital for fostering healthier relationships.

The Attraction to the Unavailable: A Familiar Dynamic

Emotionally unavailable partners often possess qualities that seem appealing on the surface, but their inability to fully engage in a relationship can echo the emotional distance experienced in childhood. For many daughters of absent fathers, this pattern becomes a way to recreate familiar dynamics, albeit in a detrimental manner. The allure of emotionally unavailable partners may stem from a desire for love and validation that remains unmet from their childhood experiences.

Take, for instance, the story of Emma. Raised in a household where her father's absence was felt profoundly, Emma grew accustomed to feelings of longing and unfulfilled expectations. As an adult, she found herself repeatedly attracted to partners who were charming yet distant - men who were often preoccupied with their careers, hobbies, or previous relationships. Emma's experiences with these partners mirrored her childhood feelings of inadequacy, as she tried to earn their affection and attention. Each relationship left her feeling more frustrated and unworthy, reinforcing the belief that love was something to be earned rather than given freely.

The Cycle of Rejection and Validation

Daughters like Emma often engage in a cyclical pattern of dating emotionally unavailable partners that is fraught with emotional highs and lows. Initially, the thrill of being chosen by someone who appears elusive can provide a temporary sense of validation. However, as the relationship unfolds, the reality of their partner's emotional unavailability becomes apparent. The inevitable emotional distance leads to feelings of rejection and frustration, creating a vicious cycle where the daughter finds herself pursuing validation from partners who cannot provide the emotional support she craves.

In her quest for love, Emma often felt a deep sense of excitement when her emotionally distant partner showed even the slightest sign of affection. However, these moments were typically short-lived, followed by periods of withdrawal. Each instance of emotional unavailability reinforced Emma's feelings of unworthiness, leading her to work harder to gain her partner's approval. This cycle perpetuated a sense of desperation that left her feeling more isolated and misunderstood.

Fear of Vulnerability: A Double-Edged Sword

The attraction to emotionally unavailable partners often stems from a profound fear of vulnerability. For daughters who have experienced abandonment or emotional neglect, the prospect of opening up to another person can feel terrifying. By choosing partners who are emotionally unavailable, they create a scenario where they can maintain a semblance of control. This allows them to avoid true intimacy while still engaging in a relationship.

Consider the case of Sarah, who, like many daughters of absent fathers, developed a fear of vulnerability. When faced with emotionally available partners, she would often feel overwhelmed by the prospect of emotional intimacy. In response, Sarah gravitated toward partners who were distant or emotionally unavailable, as these relationships allowed her to maintain a barrier. While she craved connection, her fear of being hurt often outweighed her desire for closeness. This coping mechanism provided her with an illusion of safety but ultimately resulted in loneliness and dissatisfaction.

The Impact on Self-Identity and Growth

The pattern of dating emotionally unavailable partners can also have a profound impact on a daughter's self-identity and personal growth. When a significant amount of energy is invested in trying to make an emotionally unavailable partner meet their needs, it can lead to a sense of stagnation. Daughters may find themselves neglecting their own goals, aspirations, and emotional well-being in the pursuit of love from someone who may never fully reciprocate.

Emily, another example, had dreams of pursuing higher education and establishing a fulfilling career. However, her focus became consumed by her relationship with an emotionally unavailable partner. As she invested time and energy into the relationship, her own ambitions took a backseat. This neglect contributed to a growing sense of frustration and regret, as Emily felt trapped in a cycle of seeking validation from a partner who could not provide the emotional connection she desperately desired. The consequences were twofold: she not only lost sight of her own goals but also began to internalize the belief that her worth was tied to her partner's perception of her.

Breaking the Cycle: Paths to Healing

Recognizing and breaking the cycle of dating emotionally unavailable partners is essential for healing and personal growth. Daughters who have experienced father absence can benefit from self-reflection and therapeutic support to explore their patterns and underlying fears. By addressing the root causes of their attraction to emotionally unavailable partners, they can begin to make healthier choices in their relationships.

Therapy can be a powerful tool for uncovering the emotional scars left by father absence. Through guided exploration, daughters can learn to understand their fears and insecurities, allowing them to challenge maladaptive patterns of behavior. Support groups or counseling can also provide a safe space for sharing experiences and learning from others who have faced similar challenges.

Furthermore, cultivating self-awareness can empower daughters to identify emotionally available partners who can offer the support and love they desire. By setting boundaries and prioritizing their own emotional well-being, daughters can gradually shift their focus from seeking validation through relationships to fostering a sense of self-worth that is independent of external approval.

Redefining Relationships

The patterns of dating emotionally unavailable partners reveal the complexities of love and connection for daughters raised without a father figure. The interplay of attraction, fear of vulnerability, and the struggle for self-identity creates a challenging landscape in their romantic lives. However, through self-awareness, reflection, and therapeutic support, these daughters can redefine their relationship narratives.

By understanding their past experiences and the impact of father absence, daughters can break free from the cycle of seeking love in emotionally unavailable partners. This journey toward healing not only fosters healthier relationships but also empowers them to reclaim their sense of self-worth, paving the way for fulfilling connections built on mutual trust and emotional intimacy. Ultimately, the path to healing is one of transformation, where daughters can learn to embrace vulnerability and build relationships that enrich their lives, rather than limit them.

Chapter 7:

Self-esteem and Identity Struggles

A. How Self-Worth Is Impacted by Father Absence

The absence of a father can leave an indelible mark on a daughter's sense of self-worth and identity. This impact is not merely a transient phase of childhood but a long-term consequence that shapes various aspects of a daughter's life as she transitions into adulthood. Understanding the complexities of how father absence affects self-esteem is crucial in grasping the broader implications of emotional and psychological development.

The Foundation of Self-Worth

Self-worth is often constructed during formative years, heavily influenced by familial relationships, particularly the bond between a father and daughter. Fathers play a pivotal role in affirming their daughters' value, often serving as their first role models. Through interactions, a father's presence - marked by encouragement, validation, and unconditional love - helps build a solid foundation for a daughter's self-esteem. When that presence is missing, daughters frequently experience a vacuum of affirmation that leads to feelings of inadequacy.

Consider the story of Lucy, a young woman whose father left when she was just five years old. In her formative years, she sought validation from various sources - teachers, friends, and romantic partners - yet none could fill the void left by her father. Each time Lucy encountered failure or rejection, she internalized these experiences, leading her to believe that she was not worthy of love or success. This pattern of thought became entrenched, shaping her identity and driving her to question her inherent value.

The Comparison Trap

Daughters of absent fathers often find themselves ensnared in the "comparison trap," where they measure their worth against others. This behavior can stem from the desire to prove themselves and seek validation in the absence of paternal approval. Lucy often compared herself to her peers, whose fathers were actively involved in their lives. She would notice the support and encouragement they received, which only heightened her feelings of inadequacy. Such comparisons can be damaging, leading to a distorted sense of self and reinforcing the belief that one must earn love and respect through accomplishments.

The consequences of these comparisons extend beyond self-esteem. As daughters perceive themselves as less valuable than their peers, they may develop a fixed mindset, leading them to avoid challenges for fear of failure. This avoidance further hinders personal growth and reinforces a negative self-image. Over time, this cycle can erode a daughter's confidence, limiting her ability to pursue opportunities or take risks.

Internalizing Abandonment

The emotional scars left by father absence often manifest as a profound sense of abandonment. Daughters may internalize their father's absence as a reflection of their worth, believing they were somehow unlovable or undeserving. This internalization can create a deep-rooted sense of unworthiness that lingers into adulthood, influencing relationships and personal aspirations.

For example, Emma struggled with feelings of abandonment throughout her life. As she navigated adulthood, every setback, whether in her career or relationships, reignited those childhood wounds. Each failure became a painful reminder of her father's absence, further reinforcing her belief that she was unworthy of success or love. This vicious cycle made it challenging for her to build meaningful connections with others or pursue her dreams with confidence.

Seeking Validation from Others

In an effort to combat feelings of unworthiness, daughters of absent fathers often seek validation from external sources. This need for affirmation can lead to unhealthy relationships, as these daughters may attach their self-worth to the approval of others. The desire for recognition can push them to prioritize others' needs over their own, resulting in self-neglect and the erosion of personal boundaries.

Sophie's journey illustrates this dynamic. Throughout her adult life, she found herself in relationships where she sought constant validation from her partners. Each compliment or affirmation became a fleeting source of self-worth, leading her to overlook her own needs and desires. This dependency on others for validation ultimately left her feeling empty and dissatisfied, reinforcing her initial beliefs of inadequacy.

The Quest for Identity

Father absence can profoundly disrupt a daughter's journey toward self-discovery and identity formation. The absence of a father figure often leaves a void that can complicate the process of understanding one's self and one's place in the world. Daughters may struggle to define their identity without the foundational support that a father typically provides, leading to feelings of confusion and disorientation.

As she navigated her twenties, Julia grappled with her identity. Lacking a paternal figure to guide her, she struggled to articulate her values, aspirations, and beliefs. This uncertainty manifested in her relationships, career choices, and personal goals, leading to a sense of aimlessness. Julia's quest for identity became a daunting journey marked by experimentation and frustration, as she sought to forge a sense of self in the absence of a crucial guiding influence.

The Role of Healing and Self-Discovery

Despite the challenges posed by father absence, healing is possible. Recognizing the impact of a father's absence on self-esteem and identity is the first step toward recovery. Therapy and support groups can provide a nurturing environment where daughters can explore their feelings and develop healthier coping mechanisms. Through these avenues, they can learn to disentangle their self-worth from their experiences of abandonment.

Empowerment through self-discovery is another crucial aspect of healing. Daughters can benefit from engaging in activities that foster self-exploration, such as journaling, pursuing hobbies, and setting personal goals. These practices can help them reconnect with their values and passions, gradually rebuilding their self-esteem.

Reclaiming Self-Worth

The impact of father absence on a daughter's self-worth and identity is profound and complex. The intertwining effects of abandonment, comparison, and the quest for validation create a challenging landscape for daughters as they navigate adulthood. However, the journey toward healing is attainable. By acknowledging the wounds left by father absence and actively working toward self-discovery and empowerment, daughters can reclaim their self-worth and cultivate a strong, authentic identity.

Ultimately, understanding how father absence shapes self-esteem is crucial for fostering healthier relationships and personal growth. As daughters confront their past and engage in self-reflection, they can transcend the limitations imposed by their experiences and embrace their inherent value as individuals. The path to reclaiming self-worth is not only a journey of healing but also a transformative experience that allows daughters to redefine their identities and find fulfillment in their lives.

B. Struggles with Self-Identity, Insecurity, and Seeking External Validation

The journey of self-identity is intricate, often defined by the relationships and experiences that shape a person's sense of self. For many daughters who grow up in the absence of a father, this journey becomes a labyrinth of insecurity and external validation. These women often grapple with understanding who they are, what they value, and how they fit into the world. The absence of a paternal figure can significantly complicate this quest, leading to an ongoing struggle with self-identity and a persistent need for affirmation from outside sources.

The Void of Identity Formation

In the absence of a father, daughters frequently encounter a void that complicates their identity formation. Fathers often serve as significant role models, influencing daughters' perspectives on gender roles, self-worth, and interpersonal relationships. When a father is absent, daughters may find themselves without a compass to navigate these critical aspects of their identity, leading to a sense of confusion and disorientation.

Take Mia, for example. Growing up with her father missing from her life, she often felt adrift in a sea of expectations and societal norms. While her mother did her best to provide guidance, Mia found herself questioning her value, interests, and ambitions. This lack of direction manifested in her adult relationships, where she often felt like an imposter - unworthy of love and respect. The absence of her father left her grappling with her identity, seeking to fill the gaps in her self-perception through the eyes of others.

The Weight of Insecurity

The struggles with self-identity often breed insecurity, which can become a defining characteristic of adult daughters raised without a father. Insecurity manifests as a pervasive sense of doubt regarding one's abilities, appearance, and desirability. These feelings can lead to a negative self-image that permeates various aspects of life, from professional endeavors to personal relationships.

In her early twenties, Claire faced an uphill battle against her insecurities. Despite her intelligence and creativity, she often found herself second-guessing her worth. This self-doubt was rooted in her father's absence; she had grown up believing that if her father didn't value her enough to stay, how could anyone else? This internal narrative kept her from pursuing opportunities, leading to a cycle of missed chances and increased feelings of inadequacy.

The Quest for External Validation

In a world where self-worth is often measured against societal expectations, many daughters of absent fathers develop a compulsive need for external validation. This quest for approval can lead them to seek affirmation from peers, partners, or even strangers, in a desperate attempt to fill the void left by their fathers. While external validation can provide temporary relief, it often exacerbates feelings of insecurity and unworthiness in the long run.

Consider the case of Nina, who navigated through relationships with an overwhelming need for approval. She poured her energy into making others happy, often at the expense of her own needs. In romantic relationships, she would become hyper-attuned to her partner's emotions, always seeking reassurance that she was loved and valued. While her partners initially provided the validation she craved, the reliance on external approval made her feel even more isolated when those affirmations were not forthcoming. This cycle left her feeling drained and unfulfilled, reinforcing her insecurities.

The Impact on Relationships

The struggle with self-identity and the reliance on external validation can significantly impact the nature of relationships. Women raised without fathers may find themselves in relationships characterized by dependency, where their self-worth hinges on their partner's approval. This dependency can lead to a lack of assertiveness, making it challenging for them to voice their needs or desires.

Sarah, for instance, often found herself in relationships where she felt overshadowed. In her quest for validation, she prioritized her partner's needs above her own, leading to resentment and emotional disconnection. Sarah's inability to assert herself stemmed from her childhood experiences; her father's absence had conditioned her to believe that love was conditional and that she must earn it through compliance. This dynamic created a cycle of unfulfilling relationships, each reinforcing her feelings of insecurity and self-doubt.

The Path to Self-Discovery

Despite the challenges posed by the absence of a father, the journey toward self-discovery and empowerment is possible. Acknowledging the impact of father absence on one's self-identity is the first step toward healing. Engaging in self-reflection, therapy, and supportive communities can help daughters navigate their feelings of insecurity and learn to cultivate a sense of self that is independent of external validation.

Empowerment through self-exploration is a crucial aspect of this journey. Daughters can benefit from identifying their interests, passions, and values outside the realm of societal expectations.

Journaling, pursuing hobbies, and setting personal goals can aid in rebuilding their self-esteem and fostering a more authentic sense of self.

Building Healthy Boundaries

As daughters work to redefine their self-identity, establishing healthy boundaries is essential. Learning to communicate needs and desires assertively can help them navigate relationships without compromising their sense of self-worth. Building boundaries not only fosters healthier interactions with others but also reinforces the understanding that self-worth is innate and not contingent upon external approval.

Jessica, who had struggled for years with her identity and need for validation, began to recognize the importance of boundaries in her relationships. Through therapy, she learned to express her feelings openly and assertively. This newfound ability allowed her to engage in healthier, more balanced relationships, empowering her to cultivate her self-worth independent of others' perceptions.

Embracing Authenticity

The journey of self-identity and self-worth for daughters raised without a father is undoubtedly complex, marked by struggles with insecurity and a tendency to seek validation from external sources. However, through self-awareness, empowerment, and the establishment of healthy boundaries, these daughters can reclaim their identities and foster a genuine sense of self.

Embracing authenticity becomes the guiding principle on this journey, allowing them to forge a path that honors their true selves rather than the expectations imposed by others. Ultimately, the process of healing from the absence of a father can lead to profound self-discovery, enabling daughters to redefine their identities and cultivate a sense of self-worth that is resilient, authentic, and deeply rooted in their individuality. Through this journey, they can emerge not only as survivors of their experiences but as empowered individuals who celebrate their unique identities.

C. Career Implications and Fear of Failure/Success

The intersection of self-esteem, identity struggles, and career aspirations creates a complex web for daughters raised in father-absent households. The shadows of their upbringing can loom large over their professional lives, shaping their ambitions, fueling fears of both failure and success, and ultimately influencing their career trajectories.

The Influence of Paternal Absence on Career Aspirations

Father absence can profoundly impact a daughter's career aspirations. Fathers often serve as role models, guiding daughters through the nuances of ambition, self-worth, and perseverance in the professional realm. When a father is absent, this guidance is frequently replaced by uncertainty. Many daughters grow up without a clear picture of what it means to strive for success or how to navigate challenges in the workplace, leading to a lack of confidence in pursuing their career goals.

For instance, Emily, who grew up without her father, faced immense pressure when it came to defining her career path. Without his encouragement or insight, she struggled to envision a future for herself. Instead of pursuing her passion for architecture, she settled for a job in retail management, believing that it was safer and more achievable. The absence of paternal guidance left her feeling lost, unsure of her capabilities, and ultimately unfulfilled.

The Fear of Failure: An Overwhelming Barrier

The fear of failure looms large for many daughters raised without fathers. This fear is often rooted in early childhood experiences, where the absence of a father can lead to a perception that they are inherently less worthy of success. The lack of paternal support may foster a belief that they must constantly prove their value to the world, which can manifest as an overwhelming fear of failure in their professional lives.

Consider the case of Samantha, a high-achieving woman who often found herself paralyzed by the fear of failing. Despite her talent and hard work, she frequently second-guessed her decisions and hesitated to take risks in her career. This fear stemmed from her childhood, where she internalized the message that any misstep could reinforce her feelings of unworthiness. As a result, she shied away from promotions and challenging projects, opting instead for the safety of the familiar. This self-imposed limitation not only hindered her career growth but also deepened her sense of inadequacy.

The Paradox of Success: Fear of Success and Its Consequences

Interestingly, the fear of success can be just as crippling as the fear of failure for daughters from father-absent homes. For many, the prospect of success brings with it the anxiety of surpassing expectations and the burden of responsibility. This fear is often intertwined with feelings of guilt; they may fear that achieving success will alienate them from others or trigger feelings of inadequacy in peers who have not had the same opportunities.

Take the story of Lila, a talented writer whose fear of success hindered her career. As she began to gain recognition for her work, she found herself retreating from opportunities that could elevate her career. The idea of stepping into the limelight felt overwhelming, as she worried about the potential scrutiny and pressure that would accompany her success. This fear, stemming from her father's absence, manifested in self-sabotaging behaviors that prevented her from fully embracing her talent.

The Impact on Professional Relationships

Daughters raised without fathers may also struggle to establish healthy professional relationships, often characterized by distrust and difficulty in collaboration. The absence of a father figure can create a framework where they doubt their ability to form meaningful connections in the workplace. This distrust can lead to reluctance in seeking mentorship or support from colleagues, further isolating them in their career pursuits.

For example, Megan, who had always kept her distance from male colleagues, found herself missing out on valuable opportunities. Her upbringing had instilled in her a sense of caution around authority figures, particularly men. As a result, she hesitated to seek mentorship or guidance, fearing that she would be judged or dismissed. This self-imposed barrier not only stunted her professional growth but also left her feeling unsupported in an environment where collaboration and networking are crucial.

The Path to Overcoming Fears and Embracing Opportunities

Despite the challenges posed by a father's absence, there is a path forward for daughters seeking to overcome their fears and embrace career opportunities. Recognizing and addressing these fears is a critical step in transforming their relationship with success and failure. Through therapy, self-reflection, and supportive networks, these daughters can begin to reframe their narratives and cultivate a sense of self that is independent of their upbringing.

Building a supportive network of mentors and peers can play a significant role in overcoming these challenges. By seeking out positive role models and engaging with like-minded individuals, daughters can develop the confidence needed to navigate their careers more effectively. This support system can provide the encouragement and validation that may have been missing in their formative years, helping them to break free from the chains of self-doubt.

Setting Realistic Goals and Embracing Failure

Another crucial aspect of overcoming fears in the workplace involves setting realistic goals and learning to embrace failure as a part of the growth process. By breaking down career aspirations into manageable steps, daughters can reduce the overwhelming nature of their ambitions. This approach allows for gradual progress and fosters a more balanced perspective on success and failure.

Moreover, reframing failure as a learning opportunity can empower daughters to view setbacks as essential components of their career journeys. By shifting their mindset, they can cultivate resilience and adaptability, qualities that are invaluable in any professional landscape.

Redefining Success

The journey of self-esteem and identity struggles for daughters raised without a father is marked by fears of failure and success that can significantly impact their career paths. However, through self-awareness, the establishment of supportive networks, and a commitment to personal growth, these women can redefine their relationship with success and navigate their professional lives with confidence.

Embracing their unique experiences and challenges can lead to a profound understanding of their strengths and capabilities. In doing so, they not only reclaim their identities but also empower themselves to pursue fulfilling careers that align with their passions and values. Ultimately, this journey is about transformation - transforming fears into strengths, insecurities into confidence, and aspirations into achievements.

Chapter 8:

Mental Health Outcomes

A. Chronic Stress, Anxiety, and Depression in Adult Daughters

The absence of a father during critical developmental years can cast a long shadow over a daughter's mental health, leading to chronic stress, anxiety, and depression that may persist well into adulthood. These mental health challenges are not merely a result of familial voids but are often compounded by societal expectations, personal experiences, and the struggle to form stable relationships.

The Roots of Chronic Stress

Chronic stress often stems from unresolved emotional turmoil and instability during childhood. When a father figure is absent, daughters frequently experience a vacuum of support that can lead to overwhelming feelings of abandonment and insecurity. These feelings can manifest in various ways, including difficulties in managing emotions, challenges in developing healthy coping mechanisms, and a pervasive sense of unease.

For instance, consider the experience of Lisa, who grew up without her father. As a child, she internalized her father's absence as a reflection of her own worth. This belief fueled chronic stress that colored every aspect of her life. Lisa found herself constantly worried about her relationships, academics, and even her own future. The weight of these unresolved feelings often left her feeling as if she were walking on a tightrope, where any misstep could lead to disaster.

Anxiety: The Constant Companion

As chronic stress accumulates, anxiety often emerges as a persistent companion for many daughters raised without fathers. This anxiety can take various forms, from generalized worry to more severe panic attacks. The absence of a father can strip away a sense of security and stability, leaving daughters feeling vulnerable in an unpredictable world. They may grapple with fears about their self-worth and their ability to navigate relationships, careers, and even basic life challenges.

Take, for example, Sarah, who developed severe anxiety in her teenage years. Without a father figure to provide reassurance and guidance, she became acutely aware of her fears regarding rejection and inadequacy. Social situations, which should have been enjoyable, became sources of crippling anxiety. The anticipation of judgment from peers often paralyzed her, making it difficult to engage in friendships or pursue new opportunities. This anxiety spiraled, leaving her feeling isolated and trapped in a cycle of fear.

The Onset of Depression

The relationship between father absence and depression is profound and multifaceted. Many daughters experience feelings of sadness and hopelessness as they struggle to fill the emotional void left by an absent father. These feelings can be compounded by the societal stigma surrounding mental health, which may lead them to internalize their struggles rather than seek help.

For instance, Amy's journey through adulthood was marred by episodes of depression that seemed to deepen over time. The absence of her father during her formative years fostered feelings of unworthiness, leading her to believe she was undeserving of happiness. The cycle of negative self-talk and the belief that she had to carry her burdens alone contributed to her depression. She often found herself withdrawing from social activities, isolating herself further and exacerbating her mental health struggles.

The Interplay of Chronic Stress, Anxiety, and Depression

The interplay between chronic stress, anxiety, and depression creates a complex landscape that can be difficult to navigate. These conditions often feed into one another, creating a cycle of despair that is hard to break. Chronic stress may elevate anxiety levels, which in turn can lead to depressive symptoms, creating a vicious cycle that reinforces feelings of helplessness and despair.

Consider the case of Jennifer, who found herself ensnared in this cycle. Each day, the stressors of life seemed to amplify her anxiety, which would spiral into feelings of depression. Jennifer struggled to see a way out of this cycle, feeling as if she were trapped in a dark tunnel with no light at the end. The combination of these mental health issues made it challenging for her to engage in work, relationships, and self-care, leading to a sense of hopelessness about her future.

Coping Mechanisms and Resilience

While the effects of father absence can be profound, it is essential to acknowledge the potential for resilience and healing. Many daughters develop coping mechanisms that help them navigate their mental health challenges. These mechanisms may include seeking therapy, developing supportive friendships, or engaging in creative outlets as a means of expression.

Therapy can be particularly beneficial, providing a safe space for daughters to process their experiences and develop healthier coping strategies. Through therapeutic interventions, they can learn to recognize and challenge negative thought patterns that stem from their upbringing. For example, Claire found solace in cognitive-behavioral therapy, where she learned to reframe her thoughts and address her anxiety. This journey toward self-awareness allowed her to cultivate a stronger sense of identity and self-worth.

Seeking Support: Building a Community

Building a supportive community can also play a crucial role in mitigating the impacts of father absence on mental health. Establishing connections with others who share similar experiences can foster a sense of belonging and validation. Support groups, whether in-person or online, can provide a platform for sharing stories, exchanging coping strategies, and offering encouragement.

For instance, Mia discovered a support group for women who had experienced father absence. Through sharing her story and hearing others' journeys, she found a sense of camaraderie that helped her feel less alone in her struggles. This newfound community provided her with the emotional support she had long sought, empowering her to confront her mental health challenges with renewed strength.

A Path Toward Healing

The long-term consequences of father absence on mental health are profound, with chronic stress, anxiety, and depression often intertwining to create significant challenges for adult daughters. However, through self-awareness, therapy, and the establishment of supportive relationships, these women can find a path toward healing and resilience.

Ultimately, the journey involves reclaiming their narratives, recognizing their inherent worth, and developing the tools needed to navigate life's complexities. By addressing their mental health challenges head-on, daughters can cultivate a deeper understanding of themselves and their experiences, allowing them to build fulfilling lives that transcend the shadows of their past.

B. Increased Vulnerability to Substance Abuse or Risky Behaviors

The intricate tapestry of a daughter's psychological landscape is often woven with threads of past experiences, particularly those involving father absence. As they navigate their adult lives, many women face an increased vulnerability to substance abuse and other risky behaviors.

The Psychological Toll of Father Absence

The absence of a father figure during formative years can create profound psychological implications for daughters. Feelings of abandonment, low self-esteem, and emotional instability can emerge in response to this absence. Such emotional turmoil often drives individuals to seek solace in substances or risky behaviors as a coping mechanism. The allure of these escape routes may provide a temporary respite from the overwhelming emotions associated with their past.

Consider the story of Jenna, who grew up in a single-parent household after her father left when she was just a toddler. Throughout her childhood, Jenna grappled with feelings of inadequacy, believing she had to fill the void left by her father. As she transitioned into adulthood, the emotional weight became unbearable. She began to experiment with alcohol and drugs, initially viewing them as a means to escape her reality. For Jenna, substances offered a fleeting sense of relief from the pain of her past - a reprieve that ultimately spiraled into a dependency that threatened her stability.

Seeking Validation and Acceptance

In addition to emotional escape, daughters may engage in risky behaviors as a means of seeking validation and acceptance from peers. Without the nurturing influence of a father, many women struggle to develop a strong sense of self-worth and identity. This lack of foundation can lead to a desperate desire for approval, driving them toward behaviors that may not align with their values or aspirations.

Take the case of Lauren, who often found herself in toxic relationships and engaging in reckless activities to gain attention from others. The absence of her father left a significant void in her life, and she sought validation through risky behaviors, believing that the more she engaged in wild or dangerous acts, the more she would be accepted. However, this quest for acceptance only deepened her feelings of isolation and dissatisfaction, creating a cycle of poor choices that further exacerbated her struggles.

The Role of Coping Mechanisms

Coping mechanisms developed in childhood can also play a critical role in shaping how daughters respond to stressors in adulthood. Without the guidance and support typically provided by a father, many women adopt maladaptive coping strategies, such as substance use, to manage their emotions.

For instance, Sara experienced the absence of her father throughout her teenage years, leading her to rely on unhealthy coping mechanisms to deal with feelings of sadness and anger. Initially, Sara turned to binge drinking as a way to numb her emotions and fit in with her peers. However, as her reliance on alcohol grew, so did her problems - her academic performance suffered, and she faced legal issues stemming from her reckless behavior. This vicious cycle perpetuated her mental health struggles, illustrating how the absence of a father can lead to destructive coping strategies that have lasting consequences.

The Intersection of Mental Health and Substance Abuse

The interplay between mental health challenges and substance abuse is complex and often reciprocal. Daughters who have experienced father absence may grapple with anxiety, depression, or post-traumatic stress disorder (PTSD), making them more susceptible to using substances as a form of self-medication.

Rachel's story exemplifies this intersection. After her father left, she struggled with anxiety and depression, often feeling overwhelmed by her emotions. In search of relief, she turned to prescription medications, believing they would help her manage her mental health. Unfortunately, what started as an attempt to cope quickly morphed into addiction, leading to a downward spiral that impacted her relationships, career, and overall well-being.

Social Influences and Environment

The social environment in which daughters grow up can significantly impact their susceptibility to substance abuse and risky behaviors. Peer influences, availability of substances, and community norms can all contribute to the likelihood of engaging in these behaviors.

For instance, within peer groups where substance use is normalized or glamorized, daughters may feel pressured to conform. Nicole, who grew up in a neighborhood where drug use was prevalent, found herself increasingly drawn into the world of substances. The absence of her father made her vulnerable to external influences, and she began using drugs as a means of fitting in with her friends. Despite knowing the risks, Nicole felt compelled to participate, believing it was her only avenue to social acceptance.

Long-Term Consequences and Recovery

The consequences of substance abuse and risky behaviors can be long-lasting, affecting not only physical health but also emotional and psychological well-being. Many daughters find themselves entangled in a web of dependency, facing challenges that may hinder their personal and professional growth. However, acknowledging these challenges is the first step toward recovery.

Recovery from substance abuse is a complex journey, often requiring professional help, support groups, and a strong personal commitment to change. For many daughters, engaging in therapy can provide a safe space to explore the underlying issues related to their father's absence and develop healthier coping mechanisms.

Therapies such as cognitive-behavioral therapy (CBT) can empower individuals to recognize and challenge negative thought patterns, ultimately leading to more positive behaviors. Additionally, support groups can foster a sense of community and belonging, reminding daughters that they are not alone in their struggles.

Building a New Path Forward

As daughters begin to heal from the impacts of father absence, it is crucial for them to develop a robust support network that promotes positive behaviors and healthy coping strategies. This network can include friends, family members, and mental health professionals who provide encouragement and guidance throughout their journey.

Consider Mia, who, after struggling with substance abuse for years, sought therapy and began attending support group meetings. Through these resources, she not only gained insight into her struggles but also found a community of individuals who understood her experiences. As she learned to navigate her emotions without relying on substances, Mia gradually rebuilt her life, focusing on her goals and aspirations rather than her past traumas.

The Path to Healing and Resilience

The increased vulnerability to substance abuse and risky behaviors among daughters raised without fathers underscores the profound impact of father absence on mental health outcomes. While the path to healing may be fraught with challenges, it is essential for daughters to recognize their strength and resilience. By seeking help, building supportive communities, and developing healthier coping strategies, these women can reclaim their lives and create a future that honors their journey toward healing.

In recognizing the interplay between their past experiences and present choices, daughters can break free from the cycles of substance abuse and forge a new path - one that embraces self-acceptance, emotional well-being, and the pursuit of fulfilling lives.

C. How Unresolved Childhood Wounds Manifest in Adult Life

The repercussions of father absence often extend far beyond childhood, echoing through the adult lives of daughters in multifaceted and sometimes devastating ways. These unresolved childhood wounds - formed through a lack of paternal presence, emotional support, and guidance - can manifest in various forms, influencing relationships, self-esteem, and overall mental health.

The Lingering Echo of Abandonment

At the heart of many issues stemming from father absence lies the profound sense of abandonment that can reverberate throughout a daughter's life. This emotional wound, often rooted in feelings of unworthiness and rejection, can influence how women perceive themselves and their worth. In adulthood, the unresolved pain of being left behind can manifest as a pervasive fear of abandonment, which may lead to self-sabotaging behaviors in relationships.

For example, consider the story of Emily, who, after her father left when she was just five years old, grew up harboring a deep-seated belief that she was unlovable. As she entered adulthood, this belief informed her interactions with romantic partners, causing her to push people away at the first sign of conflict. The fear of being abandoned yet again overshadowed her ability to form healthy, lasting connections. Consequently, Emily found herself trapped in a cycle of short-lived relationships, each one reinforcing her belief that she was destined to be alone. This cycle illustrates how unresolved childhood wounds can have far-reaching effects, stifling emotional growth and connection.

Emotional Dysregulation and Coping Mechanisms

The absence of a father figure can also hinder emotional regulation skills, leaving daughters ill-equipped to handle stress and negative emotions. Without a paternal role model to teach emotional intelligence and coping strategies, many women struggle to navigate their feelings, often resorting to maladaptive coping mechanisms.

Sarah, for instance, grew up in a chaotic environment following her father's departure. With her mother overwhelmed and unable to provide the emotional support she needed, Sarah learned to bottle up her feelings, fearing that expressing herself would lead to further rejection. As an adult, she found herself struggling with intense emotions - ranging from anger to profound sadness - often unable to pinpoint the root of her distress. This emotional dysregulation led Sarah to rely on unhealthy coping strategies such as binge eating and impulsive spending, actions that temporarily alleviated her emotional pain but ultimately led to guilt and shame.

The Search for Identity and Validation

The journey of self-discovery is complex for many daughters who grow up without fathers. The absence of paternal guidance can leave a significant void in a daughter's quest for identity, often leading to confusion and insecurity about her place in the world. This struggle can manifest in an excessive reliance on external validation, as many women search for approval from others to compensate for the absence of paternal support.

Jessica's story exemplifies this struggle. Raised by a single mother, Jessica often felt lost and uncertain about her identity. As she navigated her teenage years, she found herself conforming to peer pressures and engaging in behaviors that did not align with her true self, all in a desperate attempt to fit in and be accepted. The lack of a father figure to provide guidance left her vulnerable to external influences, ultimately leading to a series of unhealthy friendships and relationships that exacerbated her feelings of inadequacy. This pattern of seeking validation from others is a common manifestation of unresolved childhood wounds, revealing the deep-seated desire for acceptance and belonging.

Impact on Romantic Relationships

The unresolved emotional scars of father absence frequently resurface in adult romantic relationships, where patterns of behavior established in childhood can dictate the dynamics of love and intimacy. Daughters may find themselves unconsciously reenacting their past experiences, which can lead to a cycle of unhealthy relationships characterized by fear, distrust, and insecurity.

Take the case of Mia, who found herself consistently attracted to emotionally unavailable partners. Growing up without a father, Mia developed a belief that love was synonymous with pain and disappointment. This belief influenced her choices in partners, leading her to pursue relationships with men who mirrored the emotional distance she had experienced in her youth. As a result, Mia became entangled in a series of tumultuous relationships, each one reinforcing her childhood belief that she was unworthy of healthy, fulfilling love. This pattern highlights how unresolved childhood wounds can shape adult romantic dynamics, perpetuating a cycle of emotional distress.

Anxiety and Depression

The emotional burden of unresolved childhood wounds often manifests as anxiety and depression in adulthood. The lack of a supportive father figure can create feelings of isolation and loneliness, leading to heightened emotional vulnerability. These mental health challenges can be further exacerbated by unhealthy coping mechanisms and the ongoing struggle to navigate relationships.

Laura, for instance, faced chronic anxiety and recurrent bouts of depression in her adult life, stemming from her father's absence during her formative years. Despite her intelligence and capabilities, Laura often felt overwhelmed by a sense of impending doom, as though her past would inevitably dictate her future. The absence of a stable paternal figure left her feeling unanchored, leading to pervasive thoughts of inadequacy and fear. This emotional turmoil affected every aspect of her life, from her professional ambitions to her social interactions, illustrating the profound impact of unresolved childhood wounds on mental health.

The Path to Healing and Resolution

Recognizing and addressing the effects of unresolved childhood wounds is a crucial step toward healing and growth. Many daughters find that therapy and support groups provide invaluable spaces for exploring their past experiences and developing healthier coping strategies. Through therapy, individuals can unpack the emotional baggage carried from childhood and learn to establish healthier patterns of behavior.

Cognitive-behavioral therapy (CBT) has proven particularly effective in helping women challenge negative thought patterns associated with their pasts. By reframing their narratives and developing healthier coping mechanisms, daughters can begin to heal the wounds of their childhood and forge a more positive path forward.

In addition, building supportive relationships in adulthood can play a significant role in the healing process. By surrounding themselves with individuals who provide emotional support and encouragement, women can cultivate a sense of belonging that counters feelings of isolation and inadequacy.

A Journey Toward Wholeness

The manifestations of unresolved childhood wounds in adult life can be profound and far-reaching, influencing emotional well-being, relationships, and self-identity. However, acknowledging these wounds is the first step on the path to healing. By engaging in therapeutic practices, fostering supportive relationships, and challenging negative beliefs, daughters can work toward transforming their pain into empowerment.

While the scars of father absence may never fully disappear, the journey toward wholeness and self-acceptance is possible. As daughters learn to navigate their emotions, build healthier relationships, and cultivate a strong sense of identity, they can reclaim their lives and break free from the cycles of pain, ultimately embracing a future filled with hope and resilience.

Chapter 9:

Recognizing the Wounds

A. Acknowledging the Emotional Scars Left by an Absent Father

The journey toward healing begins with the painful yet necessary process of recognizing the wounds that father absence has inflicted. For many daughters, acknowledging these emotional scars is often the most challenging step in their quest for self-acceptance and recovery. The profound impact of an absent father can create a complex web of emotions that includes anger, sadness, shame, and confusion. Understanding and confronting these feelings is critical for personal growth and empowerment, as it allows individuals to process their past and begin the journey toward emotional healing.

The Complexity of Emotions

When a father is absent, the emotional fallout can be intricate and multifaceted. Daughters may grapple with conflicting feelings: love for the father who was absent, anger at the pain of his absence, and sadness over the missed opportunities for connection. These emotions can manifest in various ways, often creating an internal struggle that hinders emotional development.

For instance, Sarah found herself oscillating between longing for her father's love and feeling resentful for the years of neglect. This inner conflict left her feeling fragmented, unable to fully embrace the positive aspects of her life. The complexity of her emotions underscored the necessity of recognizing and validating her feelings, rather than suppressing them. In doing so, Sarah began to understand that her feelings were legitimate responses to her experiences and not signs of weakness or failure.

The Role of Social Stigmas

In a society that often emphasizes the importance of a father's role, the absence of one can carry a heavy stigma. Daughters of absent fathers may internalize societal judgments, feeling compelled to hide their pain or downplay their experiences. This suppression of emotions can lead to a dangerous cycle of shame and silence, further complicating the process of healing.

Lisa, for example, felt the pressure to conform to societal norms that dictated a "perfect" family image. She often minimized her feelings of hurt and inadequacy, fearing that expressing her pain would invite judgment or pity. By recognizing the stigma surrounding father absence, Lisa learned to advocate for her own emotional truth, allowing her to break free from the constraints of societal expectations.

The Importance of Self-Reflection

Acknowledging the emotional scars left by an absent father requires a deep and often painful self-reflection process. This reflection can be facilitated through journaling, therapy, or open conversations with trusted individuals. Engaging in self-reflection allows daughters to explore their feelings and experiences, making sense of the complex emotions associated with their father's absence.

For example, Michelle began journaling as a way to navigate her feelings of abandonment. Through her writing, she unearthed memories of her father that she had long buried, confronting the pain that came with them. This act of self-exploration provided Michelle with clarity and insight, enabling her to articulate her feelings and understand their roots. The practice of self-reflection served not only as a tool for recognizing her wounds but also as a pathway to self-discovery and acceptance.

The Impact of Acknowledgment

The act of acknowledging emotional scars is not merely an exercise in self-pity; rather, it serves as a powerful catalyst for healing. When daughters confront their pain, they can begin to take ownership of their narratives, transforming their experiences into sources of strength. Acknowledgment allows for the release of pent-up emotions, leading to a sense of liberation and empowerment.

For instance, after years of grappling with her father's absence, Emma attended a support group for women with similar experiences. In sharing her story, she found a sense of community and validation that she had longed for. The acknowledgment of her pain, both by herself and by others who understood, fostered a healing environment where she could openly discuss her feelings without fear of judgment. This communal recognition played a pivotal role in Emma's journey toward healing, as she learned to embrace her scars as part of her unique story.

The Path to Forgiveness

Acknowledging emotional scars often opens the door to the difficult but essential journey of forgiveness. Forgiveness does not necessarily mean condoning the actions of an absent father but rather liberating oneself from the grip of anger and resentment. This process can be profoundly transformative, allowing daughters to reclaim their power and agency.

Clara, for example, struggled for years with feelings of anger toward her father for abandoning her and her mother. Through therapy, she began to understand that holding onto this anger was ultimately hindering her personal growth. By working through her feelings, Clara was able to forgive her father - not for his sake, but for her own. This act of forgiveness did not erase her pain, but it allowed her to move forward with a lighter heart and a greater sense of control over her life.

Building Resilience

Recognizing and acknowledging emotional scars fosters resilience, empowering daughters to confront challenges with newfound strength and insight. By understanding the roots of their pain, women can develop strategies for coping with stress, anxiety, and relationship issues that may arise as a result of their father's absence.

Maria, who had spent years feeling inadequate in her relationships, found that acknowledging her past experiences equipped her with the tools to navigate her emotional landscape. She learned to communicate her needs effectively, set boundaries, and practice self-compassion. This resilience became a protective factor, enabling her to cultivate healthier relationships and embrace her worth.

The Journey of Healing

The process of acknowledging the emotional scars left by an absent father is both a painful and transformative journey. It requires courage, vulnerability, and a commitment to self-discovery. As daughters face their feelings, confront societal stigmas, and engage in self-reflection, they can begin to understand and accept the complexities of their emotions.

Through acknowledgment comes empowerment. By recognizing their wounds, daughters can reclaim their narratives and embark on a path toward healing, forgiveness, and resilience. This journey is not linear; it is filled with ups and downs, triumphs and setbacks. Yet, each step taken toward recognizing and embracing their emotional scars ultimately leads to a brighter, more authentic existence, where they can redefine their identities and foster meaningful connections with themselves and others.

B. Importance of Facing These Challenges Without Avoidance or Denial

In the journey toward healing, one of the most crucial yet daunting tasks is confronting the emotional wounds left by an absent father. This confrontation demands courage and resilience, as it involves acknowledging the hurt and pain that may have been suppressed or avoided. The tendency to seek refuge in avoidance or denial can feel comforting in the short term but ultimately stunts emotional growth and prolongs suffering. Understanding the importance of facing these challenges head-on is essential for reclaiming one's narrative, fostering healing, and building a foundation for a more fulfilling life.

The Dangers of Avoidance

Avoidance, whether through distraction, denial, or repression, creates a false sense of security. In the short term, it may appear easier to sidestep uncomfortable emotions, but this strategy can lead to deeper emotional turmoil in the long run. When individuals avoid confronting their feelings, they risk perpetuating a cycle of pain that manifests in various detrimental ways - such as anxiety, depression, and difficulties in relationships.

For example, Anna found herself constantly busy with work and social activities, believing that staying preoccupied would shield her from the emotional pain of her father's absence. However, this avoidance strategy only served to mask her feelings. Whenever she found herself in a quiet moment, memories of her father would surface, flooding her with emotions she was not prepared to face. This internal conflict ultimately led Anna to experience chronic anxiety and a sense of emptiness, revealing that avoidance was not the safe harbor she had hoped it would be.

The Role of Denial in Emotional Growth

Denial, akin to avoidance, offers a temporary reprieve from facing harsh realities. While it may provide immediate relief, it prevents individuals from engaging with their emotions and understanding their impact on their lives. Denying the influence of an absent father can lead to distorted perceptions of self-worth, relationships, and emotional health.

For instance, when Kelly discovered her father's absence had shaped her self-image, she struggled with feelings of unworthiness. Initially, she denied that her father's absence had any significant effect on her life, telling herself she was strong enough to overcome it. However, as she delved deeper into her experiences, she recognized that denying her father's impact only fueled her insecurity. It was only when she confronted this denial that Kelly could begin to understand her patterns in relationships and work toward healing.

The Benefits of Confrontation

Facing emotional challenges requires immense courage, but the benefits of such confrontation are transformative. When individuals commit to facing their feelings rather than running from them, they open the door to self-discovery and growth. Confrontation allows for the exploration of emotions in a safe space, leading to greater understanding and acceptance of oneself.

For example, during her therapy sessions, Michelle learned to articulate her feelings about her father's absence. Initially, it felt overwhelming; however, as she continued to express her emotions, she began to experience a profound sense of relief. She realized that articulating her feelings helped her make sense of the complexities of her experiences. This confrontation became a pivotal moment in her healing journey, enabling her to embrace her past and build a stronger sense of self.

Cultivating Emotional Resilience

Confronting emotional wounds strengthens resilience. By facing challenges head-on, individuals develop coping mechanisms and emotional tools that serve them well in other areas of life. The skills learned through this process - such as emotional regulation, self-compassion, and effective communication - become invaluable assets in navigating future hardships.

Samantha, for example, learned to articulate her needs and feelings effectively after confronting her father's absence. This newfound resilience allowed her to establish healthier boundaries in her relationships, reducing conflict and fostering more meaningful connections. Instead of shying away from difficult conversations, she embraced them as opportunities for growth. The transformation she experienced was a testament to the power of facing emotional challenges rather than avoiding them.

Creating Space for Healing

Creating space for healing involves allowing oneself to feel and process difficult emotions. This space can be facilitated through various methods, including journaling, therapy, support groups, or creative expression. By giving oneself permission to grieve the absence of a father, individuals can begin to reclaim their stories and embark on a path toward healing.

For instance, during her artistic endeavors, Julia discovered that painting became a therapeutic outlet for expressing her emotions surrounding her father's absence. Each brushstroke allowed her to explore feelings she had previously buried. Through this creative process, she transformed her pain into something beautiful, illustrating the importance of giving oneself the space to heal.

Building a Support System

Confronting emotional challenges can be daunting, and having a supportive network can make a significant difference. Sharing one's experiences with trusted friends or family members provides validation and helps alleviate feelings of isolation. Support groups or therapy also offer safe environments for individuals to express their feelings and gain insights from others who have experienced similar struggles.

For example, after joining a support group for daughters of absent fathers, Emily found solace in the stories shared by others. The camaraderie created a safe space where she could express her pain without fear of judgment. This support system not only validated her feelings but also encouraged her to confront her past actively. Emily's experience demonstrated how powerful a community could be in fostering healing and resilience.

Embracing Vulnerability

Facing emotional challenges without avoidance or denial requires embracing vulnerability. While vulnerability can feel intimidating, it is essential for personal growth and connection. By allowing oneself to be vulnerable, individuals open the door to authentic experiences, genuine relationships, and the possibility of healing.

For instance, when Lisa decided to share her story of her father's absence with a close friend, she felt an initial wave of fear. However, she soon discovered that this act of vulnerability fostered a deeper connection with her friend, who also had faced similar struggles. Embracing vulnerability transformed Lisa's experience, allowing her to cultivate deeper, more meaningful relationships built on mutual understanding and empathy.

The Path Forward

The importance of facing emotional challenges without avoidance or denial cannot be overstated. While the road to confrontation may be fraught with discomfort and vulnerability, it is ultimately a path toward healing and empowerment. By acknowledging the wounds left by an absent father, individuals reclaim their narratives, develop emotional resilience, and build healthier relationships.

Through facing these challenges, daughters can cultivate a greater understanding of themselves, learn valuable coping strategies, and embrace the full spectrum of their emotional experiences. In doing so, they not only honor their past but also pave the way for a more fulfilling and authentic future, where they can thrive despite their histories. The journey may be long and arduous, but with each step taken toward facing their emotional wounds, they move closer to a place of healing and self-acceptance.

Chapter 10:

Healing the Father Wound

A. Therapeutic Approaches: Counseling, Journaling, and Self-Awareness Exercises

Healing the wounds left by an absent father is a profound journey that requires intention, courage, and a multifaceted approach to therapy. Each individual's experience is unique, and what works for one person may not resonate with another. Therefore, employing a variety of therapeutic techniques - such as counseling, journaling, and self-awareness exercises - can provide the comprehensive support needed to navigate the complexities of father wounds. Understanding and utilizing these approaches can lead to emotional healing, self-discovery, and ultimately, a more fulfilling life.

The Role of Counseling in Healing

Counseling is often one of the most effective avenues for addressing the emotional scars left by an absent father. A trained therapist can provide a safe and supportive environment where individuals can explore their feelings, thoughts, and behaviors associated with their experiences. Through various modalities - such as cognitive-behavioral therapy (CBT), psychodynamic therapy, and family systems therapy - clients can gain insights into how their father's absence has shaped their lives.

For example, CBT focuses on identifying and changing negative thought patterns. In counseling sessions, Lisa learned to challenge the beliefs she held about herself due to her father's absence. Through guided exercises, she began to recognize how these beliefs affected her self-esteem and relationships. The therapist helped her reframe her thoughts, gradually replacing self-criticism with self-compassion. This shift in perspective allowed Lisa to break free from the limiting beliefs that had kept her emotionally confined.

Exploring Emotional Depths Through Journaling

Journaling is another powerful therapeutic tool that encourages emotional exploration and self-reflection. Writing about feelings and experiences provides a private outlet for processing complex emotions related to an absent father. This practice not only helps in articulating feelings but also allows for the exploration of memories, patterns, and the impact of those experiences on one's identity.

Julia, for instance, found that journaling became an essential part of her healing process. Every evening, she dedicated time to writing about her day, her feelings, and the lingering thoughts about her father. This practice opened a pathway for Julia to confront emotions she had long suppressed - anger, sadness, and confusion. As she penned her thoughts, she discovered recurring themes in her writing, such as feelings of abandonment and a yearning for connection. Journaling provided Julia with clarity and a sense of relief, as she felt less burdened by her unexpressed emotions.

Moreover, journaling can also serve as a record of growth and progress. By revisiting past entries, individuals can witness their emotional evolution, celebrating milestones and recognizing patterns of change. This retrospective view can be incredibly empowering, reinforcing the notion that healing is indeed a journey marked by resilience and courage.

Cultivating Self-Awareness Through Exercises

Self-awareness exercises play a pivotal role in healing the father wound by promoting introspection and personal insight. These exercises can take various forms, including mindfulness practices, guided visualizations, and reflective prompts. By cultivating self-awareness, individuals can better understand their emotional triggers, patterns of behavior, and the influence of their father's absence on their lives.

For example, mindfulness meditation encourages individuals to observe their thoughts and feelings without judgment. During a mindfulness session, Samantha discovered that many of her thoughts were rooted in her father's absence. As she practiced being present with her emotions, she noticed a tendency to self-sabotage in relationships. This realization prompted her to explore these patterns further, leading to deeper discussions with her therapist. By gaining insight into her emotional landscape, Samantha felt more empowered to make conscious choices in her relationships, rather than reacting from a place of pain.

Additionally, guided visualizations can be instrumental in connecting with one's inner child - the part of the self that may have been wounded by the absence of a father. During one session, Anna was guided to envision her younger self and to speak words of affirmation and love to that child. This exercise allowed her to confront feelings of abandonment and to nurture her inner self with kindness and compassion. The experience of connecting with her inner child fostered a sense of healing and reconciliation with her past.

Building a Supportive Environment

Creating a supportive environment is crucial for anyone embarking on the journey of healing the father wound. Whether through counseling, journaling, or self-awareness exercises, having a network of understanding friends, family, or support groups can enhance the healing process. Sharing experiences and insights with others who have faced similar challenges can provide validation, encouragement, and a sense of belonging.

For instance, after attending a support group focused on healing father wounds, Emily felt an overwhelming sense of relief. Hearing others share their stories allowed her to see that she was not alone in her struggles. The group became a safe space where she could express her feelings openly, and in turn, listen to the journeys of others. The mutual support fostered a sense of community, reinforcing the idea that healing is a shared endeavor.

Embracing the Healing Process

Healing the father wound is not a linear journey; it is a process filled with ups and downs. Understanding that setbacks are a natural part of the healing journey can help individuals maintain hope and perseverance. Each step taken - whether through counseling, journaling, or self-awareness exercises - contributes to the overall healing process. Embracing the complexities of emotions, rather than avoiding or denying them, allows individuals to confront their past and reclaim their narratives.

For example, during her healing journey, Michelle experienced days filled with hope and progress, followed by moments of deep sorrow and longing for her father. Instead of viewing these setbacks as failures, she learned to recognize them as part of her growth. In her counseling sessions, Michelle expressed her feelings of frustration and sadness, only to discover that these emotions were valid responses to her experiences. This understanding encouraged her to embrace the full spectrum of her feelings and to be gentle with herself during challenging moments.

The Path to Healing

Healing the father wound requires a comprehensive approach that encompasses counseling, journaling, and self-awareness exercises. Each of these therapeutic techniques offers unique benefits that contribute to emotional healing and personal growth. By engaging with these practices, individuals can explore their feelings, confront their past, and ultimately pave the way for a more fulfilling life.

As individuals embark on this journey, it is essential to remember that healing is not a destination but a lifelong process. Through patience, self-compassion, and commitment, daughters can begin to unravel the complexities of their experiences and embrace the possibility of renewal. By acknowledging their wounds and actively working toward healing, they can reclaim their narratives and create a brighter future, marked by resilience, self-love, and emotional freedom.

B. How Daughters Can Begin to Heal and Create a Sense of Closure

The journey toward healing the father wound is profoundly personal and often challenging, yet it holds the promise of transformation and growth. Daughters who have felt the absence of their fathers may find themselves grappling with a myriad of emotions, from grief and anger to confusion and longing. However, by actively engaging in processes that foster healing and closure, they can reclaim their narratives, reshape their identities, and move toward a future defined not by their past wounds but by resilience and strength.

Acknowledging Emotions as a First Step

The initial step in the healing process often involves acknowledging the emotions associated with the father wound. For many daughters, the absence of a father can create a complex emotional landscape filled with feelings of abandonment, sadness, and inadequacy. It is crucial to recognize that these emotions are valid and deserve attention. By confronting feelings head-on rather than burying them, daughters can begin to understand the impact of their father's absence on their lives.

For instance, Laura, who spent years avoiding discussions about her father, eventually found herself overwhelmed by grief. In therapy, she learned to articulate her feelings, writing them down and discussing them with her therapist. This practice of acknowledgment allowed Laura to confront the pain of her father's absence, providing her with a sense of relief. By verbalizing her feelings, she took the first significant step toward healing, transforming her grief into an opportunity for growth.

Writing Letters to Their Fathers

One powerful exercise for creating a sense of closure involves writing letters to their absent fathers. This practice allows daughters to express their feelings, articulate their pain, and communicate unresolved emotions. These letters can serve as an outlet for both anger and love, as daughters reflect on what they wished they could have said or how their lives might have been different with their father present.

For example, Sarah decided to write a letter to her father, detailing the milestones he missed in her life - from her high school graduation to her wedding day. As she poured her heart onto the page, she felt a mix of sadness and catharsis. Writing this letter provided Sarah with a platform to express not only her disappointment but also her hopes for understanding and forgiveness. While she knew her father would never read it, the act of writing allowed her to confront her feelings and find closure within herself. Afterward, she chose to keep the letter in a special place, viewing it as a symbolic release of her pain.

Engaging in Rituals of Closure

Engaging in personal rituals can also be a powerful means of fostering closure. Such rituals can take various forms, from symbolic acts of letting go to commemorative events honoring the father's memory. These acts provide daughters with tangible ways to express their emotions and facilitate healing.

For instance, Anna chose to light a candle on the anniversary of her father's passing. This simple act became a meaningful ritual that allowed her to reflect on their relationship and the impact of his absence. In doing so, Anna created a space for her emotions, acknowledging both the sorrow of loss and the lessons learned from her experiences. Over time, this ritual evolved into a way for her to celebrate her growth and resilience, allowing her to transform her father's absence into a source of strength.

Therapy and Support Groups

Seeking professional support through therapy or support groups can significantly aid in the healing process. Counseling provides a safe space for daughters to explore their feelings, navigate complex emotions, and receive guidance on their journey toward closure. Additionally, support groups offer an opportunity to connect with others who have experienced similar struggles, fostering a sense of community and shared understanding.

Maria, for example, joined a support group specifically for daughters of absent fathers. In this group, she found validation and comfort in hearing the stories of others. The shared experiences allowed her to recognize her feelings as common rather than isolated, and she felt empowered by the collective journey of healing. Together, the group engaged in discussions and shared strategies for coping, creating a supportive network that reinforced Maria's resolve to heal.

Developing Healthy Coping Mechanisms

Creating healthy coping mechanisms is crucial for daughters as they navigate the emotional terrain of the father wound. Engaging in activities that promote self-care and emotional well-being can help daughters find balance and strength amid their struggles. These coping strategies can include exercise, creative expression, mindfulness practices, and pursuing hobbies that bring joy and fulfillment.

Emily discovered that practicing yoga and meditation helped her manage her anxiety and emotional turmoil. By dedicating time to self-care, she learned to cultivate a sense of inner peace and resilience. As she connected with her body and mind, she found solace in the present moment, reducing the weight of her past experiences. By prioritizing her well-being, Emily could create a healthier emotional landscape that fostered healing and closure.

Embracing Forgiveness and Letting Go

Forgiveness is often a vital component of the healing process, not only for the absent father but also for oneself. Learning to forgive can free daughters from the emotional burdens of resentment and anger, allowing them to reclaim their power and agency. This does not imply excusing the father's absence or minimizing the pain caused; rather, it is a choice to let go of the grip these feelings have on their lives.

Grace found that as she worked through her anger towards her father, she began to understand his struggles and limitations. This perspective shift allowed her to embrace forgiveness - not for his sake but for her own. In therapy, she learned that letting go of anger was a way to reclaim her narrative and prevent her father's absence from dictating her future. As she embraced forgiveness, Grace discovered a profound sense of relief, freeing her to cultivate healthier relationships and a more positive self-image.

Moving Forward with Purpose

Ultimately, healing the father wound is about moving forward with purpose and intention. As daughters begin to create closure, they can reflect on how their experiences have shaped their identities and aspirations. This process of self-discovery enables them to build a life aligned with their values and goals, free from the shadow of their past.

Sophie, for instance, decided to channel her experiences into advocacy work for other daughters of absent fathers. By sharing her story and supporting others on similar journeys, she found purpose and fulfillment. This shift in focus from pain to empowerment not only allowed Sophie to heal but also transformed her past into a source of strength and inspiration for others. Her journey became a testament to resilience, highlighting the possibility of growth even in the face of adversity.

141

The Path to Healing and Closure

Healing the father wound is a multifaceted journey that requires active engagement and a willingness to confront difficult emotions. By acknowledging feelings, writing letters, engaging in rituals, seeking support, developing healthy coping mechanisms, embracing forgiveness, and moving forward with purpose, daughters can create a sense of closure and reclaim their narratives.

The journey may not always be linear, and setbacks may occur, but each step taken toward healing is a testament to resilience and courage. By actively participating in their healing process, daughters can transform their experiences of loss and absence into a source of strength, shaping their identities and futures in meaningful ways. Ultimately, this journey allows for growth, empowerment, and the possibility of forging deeper connections with themselves and others.

C. Breaking the Cycle: Healing Through Forgiveness and Self-Love

Healing the father wound is not merely an act of acknowledging pain or reflecting on past experiences; it is a transformative journey that encompasses forgiveness and self-love. These two pivotal elements act as catalysts for breaking the cycle of hurt and empowering daughters to reclaim their lives and identities.

Understanding the Cycle of Hurt

At the heart of healing lies an understanding of the cycle of hurt that often perpetuates through generations. When a father is absent - whether physically, emotionally, or both - daughters can develop a myriad of unresolved feelings. This absence may lead to feelings of unworthiness, distrust, and insecurity that shape how they view themselves and interact with the world. Often, these negative patterns can continue into adulthood, affecting relationships and perpetuating cycles of pain. Recognizing this cycle is the first step toward breaking free from its grasp.

For many daughters, the absence of a father figure can create a void filled with feelings of inadequacy and self-doubt. Jenna, for instance, grew up believing she was not deserving of love due to her father's abandonment. As she navigated through relationships, she unconsciously chose partners who echoed her father's absence, repeating the cycle of hurt. It wasn't until she began to unpack these feelings in therapy that Jenna realized the necessity of breaking this cycle - not just for herself, but for future generations.

The Power of Forgiveness

Forgiveness is often perceived as an act of grace extended toward others, particularly those who have caused us pain. However, when it comes to healing the father wound, forgiveness can also be a gift we give to ourselves. It is not about condoning the actions of the absent father or minimizing the impact of their absence; rather, it is about liberating oneself from the chains of resentment and anger that can hinder personal growth.

The journey of forgiveness often begins with self-reflection. Daughters are encouraged to explore the feelings of anger, betrayal, and sadness that accompany their father's absence. Recognizing these emotions is essential, as it allows them to articulate their pain. For example, when Mia began to write about her father's absence, she acknowledged feelings of resentment that she had buried for years. Through this exploration, she realized that holding onto anger only hurt her, not him. This realization was pivotal in her journey toward forgiveness.

Forgiveness does not happen overnight; it is a process that requires patience and commitment. In practice, it can involve visualizing conversations with the absent father, expressing feelings of hurt and disappointment in letters, or even engaging in guided meditations focused on releasing negative emotions. During a particularly transformative session, Mia envisioned a conversation with her father where she expressed her pain, ultimately finding a sense of closure. The act of voicing her feelings was a significant step in forgiving - not just her father, but also herself for carrying the weight of that anger for so long.

The Journey of Self-Love

Self-love is equally crucial in the healing process. It is the foundation upon which daughters can build their identities, free from the limitations imposed by the absence of their fathers. Cultivating self-love involves recognizing one's worth, embracing individuality, and prioritizing personal well-being. It requires daughters to treat themselves with the same kindness and compassion they would extend to a dear friend.

For many daughters, self-love may seem elusive, particularly if they have internalized feelings of unworthiness stemming from their father's absence. It requires a conscious effort to rewire negative self-perceptions. Sarah discovered this when she started a daily self-care practice, incorporating affirmations into her routine. Each morning, she would stand before the mirror and remind herself of her strengths, accomplishments, and inherent worth. Gradually, this practice began to reshape her self-image, enabling her to confront feelings of inadequacy with confidence.

Furthermore, self-love encompasses setting boundaries and prioritizing one's needs. It means recognizing toxic patterns, whether in relationships or self-destructive behaviors, and choosing to break free from them. Anna learned to establish boundaries in her friendships, realizing that she often attracted people who mirrored her father's absence, leading to emotional turmoil. By prioritizing her well-being and surrounding herself with supportive individuals, she fostered an environment conducive to healing.

Rewriting the Narrative

Forgiveness and self-love empower daughters to rewrite their narratives, transforming their experiences of loss into stories of resilience and strength. This process involves reframing how they view their father's absence, shifting the focus from victimhood to empowerment. As daughters learn to embrace their identities, they can begin to craft a future that is defined by their choices rather than their past.

Elena's journey exemplifies this transformation. Initially burdened by feelings of abandonment, she gradually recognized that her father's absence did not dictate her value or potential. Through therapy, she learned to articulate her desires and set goals aligned with her true self. This reframing allowed Elena to pursue her dreams unapologetically, breaking the cycle of limitation imposed by her past. As she embraced her identity, she began to inspire others, turning her pain into a platform for advocacy and empowerment.

Generating New Relationships

As daughters embrace forgiveness and self-love, they often find themselves better equipped to cultivate healthier relationships. By recognizing their worth, they are less likely to tolerate behaviors that perpetuate feelings of inadequacy. This shift not only affects romantic relationships but also friendships and familial connections.

Emily's newfound sense of self-love allowed her to reevaluate her friendships, leading to the dissolution of toxic relationships that had previously drained her emotionally. Instead, she surrounded herself with supportive friends who encouraged her growth and celebrated her accomplishments. This supportive network reinforced her journey of healing, creating a positive feedback loop that encouraged further self-exploration and growth.

A Legacy of Healing

Breaking the cycle of hurt caused by the father wound requires a commitment to healing through forgiveness and self-love. By understanding the cycle of pain, actively engaging in the process of forgiveness, and cultivating a deep sense of self-worth, daughters can transform their experiences into powerful narratives of resilience. This journey not only fosters personal growth but also empowers them to create healthier relationships and legacies for future generations.

The healing journey is ongoing, marked by moments of reflection and self-discovery. It involves recognizing that the past does not define the future and that every step taken toward healing is an act of reclamation. Through forgiveness and self-love, daughters can emerge from the shadows of their father's absence, illuminating their paths with strength, authenticity, and a renewed sense of purpose. Ultimately, they can break the cycle, leaving behind a legacy of healing for themselves and generations to come.

Chapter 11:

Building Healthy Relationships with Male Figures

A. Rewriting the Script: Cultivating Healthier Relationships with Men

Building healthy relationships with male figures is a vital aspect of the healing journey for daughters who have experienced father absence. The absence of a paternal influence can create a void that affects how daughters perceive men and relate to them throughout their lives.

Understanding the Impact of Father Absence

To effectively rewrite the script, it is crucial to understand the lasting impact of father absence on daughters. The absence often leads to a distorted perception of masculinity and male relationships, creating a landscape where feelings of mistrust, fear, or unrealistic expectations can flourish. Daughters may grapple with conflicting emotions, oscillating between seeking male approval and pushing men away due to fear of rejection or abandonment.

Take, for instance, Claire, who grew up without a father. As she entered adulthood, she found herself drawn to men who mirrored her father's absence - emotionally unavailable and dismissive of her needs. Her relationships became a source of frustration and disappointment, perpetuating feelings of inadequacy and reinforcing the belief that she was unworthy of love. Recognizing this pattern was the first step in Claire's journey to rewriting her relationship script.

Identifying Patterns and Setting Intentions

The first step in rewriting the script involves identifying recurring patterns in relationships with men. Daughters must take a critical look at their past interactions and recognize the dynamics that have played out repeatedly. This self-reflection can illuminate underlying beliefs about themselves and men, offering insight into how these beliefs may have shaped their experiences.

Setting intentions for future relationships is a powerful tool for transformation. By articulating what they desire in a relationship - such as respect, honesty, and emotional support - daughters can create a blueprint for healthier connections. For Claire, this meant acknowledging her worth and committing to seeking partners who aligned with her values. By consciously choosing to prioritize relationships that foster mutual respect and support, she began to shift her focus away from fear and toward empowerment.

Building Trust and Communication Skills

Trust is a foundational element in any healthy relationship, and rebuilding it after experiencing father absence can be challenging. It often requires daughters to confront their fears and vulnerabilities head-on. Engaging in open and honest communication is essential in establishing trust with male figures.

Participating in therapy or support groups can provide a safe space for daughters to explore their feelings about men and develop their communication skills. For example, during group sessions, Emily learned the importance of expressing her needs clearly and directly. She practiced articulating her feelings and boundaries, recognizing that vulnerability could lead to stronger connections rather than rejection.

Building trust also involves recognizing that not all men will mirror the absence or negativity experienced in the past. Daughters can benefit from surrounding themselves with positive male role models - friends, mentors, or family members - who exemplify the qualities they wish to attract in a partner. By observing and engaging with these healthy relationships, daughters can redefine their understanding of masculinity and build a more positive narrative around male figures.

Embracing Vulnerability and Authenticity

Embracing vulnerability is a crucial aspect of cultivating healthy relationships with men. Many daughters may associate vulnerability with weakness, stemming from past experiences of abandonment or betrayal. However, vulnerability is the gateway to authentic connections. When daughters allow themselves to be vulnerable, they open the door to deeper emotional intimacy.

Anna discovered this during her journey of healing. Initially, she struggled to express her feelings for fear of being hurt. However, as she learned to embrace her vulnerability, she found that it strengthened her connections with men. In her newfound relationship, she expressed her fears and insecurities openly, allowing her partner to respond with compassion and understanding. This openness created a safe space for both of them, fostering a deeper bond rooted in trust.

Authenticity also plays a significant role in building healthy relationships. Daughters must embrace their true selves, recognizing that they deserve love and acceptance for who they are, not who they think they should be. This journey of self-acceptance empowers them to attract partners who appreciate them for their individuality. By engaging in activities that reflect their interests and values, daughters can meet like-minded individuals who resonate with their authentic selves.

Learning to Set Boundaries

Setting boundaries is essential for cultivating healthy relationships with men. It involves recognizing personal limits and communicating them clearly to others. Daughters who have experienced father absence may struggle with boundaries, often feeling compelled to please others at their own expense. However, healthy relationships thrive on mutual respect and understanding of personal space.

Daughters can practice setting boundaries by identifying situations or behaviors that make them uncomfortable. This process requires self-awareness and the courage to assert their needs. For instance, Sarah learned to assert her boundaries in her friendship with a male colleague who often crossed the line with inappropriate jokes. By clearly communicating her discomfort, she established a boundary that fostered respect and understanding in their relationship.

Developing Empathy and Understanding

Empathy is a powerful tool for cultivating healthy relationships with men. Daughters can benefit from developing empathy not only for themselves but also for the men in their lives. Understanding that everyone carries their own wounds and struggles can foster compassion and strengthen connections.

In her journey, Claire learned to practice empathy by seeking to understand the perspectives of the men she interacted with. Instead of viewing them through the lens of her father's absence, she began to appreciate their individuality and experiences. This shift allowed her to engage in more meaningful conversations, breaking down barriers that previously separated her from healthy relationships.

Embracing a New Narrative

Rewriting the script of relationships with male figures is a profound and transformative process for daughters healing from father absence. By identifying patterns, setting intentions, building trust, embracing vulnerability, and establishing boundaries, daughters can cultivate connections that are healthy, supportive, and enriching. This journey not only empowers them to break free from past narratives but also paves the way for healthier relationships in the future.

The work of rewriting the script is ongoing, marked by moments of reflection, growth, and discovery. Each step taken toward healthier relationships is an act of reclaiming agency and embracing self-worth. As daughters learn to navigate their connections with men, they forge a new path - one defined by respect, authenticity, and emotional intimacy. Ultimately, this journey of healing and transformation is a testament to their resilience, allowing them to create a legacy of healthy relationships for themselves and those who follow.

B. Setting Boundaries, Establishing Trust, and Practicing Emotional Vulnerability

Creating and maintaining healthy relationships with male figures requires intentional efforts to establish boundaries, foster trust, and embrace emotional vulnerability. For daughters who have experienced the impact of father absence, these elements can be particularly challenging yet essential for forming deep, meaningful connections. By understanding the significance of each aspect and learning how to implement them, daughters can transform their relationships into spaces of safety, support, and genuine connection.

The Importance of Setting Boundaries

Setting boundaries is a fundamental skill in nurturing healthy relationships. Boundaries serve as the invisible lines that define personal limits, helping individuals communicate their needs and protect their emotional well-being. For daughters who have faced the void of a father's presence, understanding how to articulate these boundaries can be a transformative experience.

Identifying Personal Limits

The first step in establishing boundaries is recognizing one's own limits. This involves reflecting on what feels comfortable or uncomfortable in interactions with men. Daughters must consider various aspects, including emotional, physical, and time boundaries. For instance, if a daughter feels overwhelmed by a friend's constant need for support, she might realize that she needs to establish a boundary around how much time she dedicates to that friendship.

Communicating Boundaries Clearly

Once personal limits are identified, the next step is clear communication. Daughters must practice expressing their boundaries

153

assertively, without fear of rejection or conflict. This might feel daunting, especially for those who have been conditioned to please others or avoid confrontation. However, open dialogue is key to building relationships that honor both parties' needs.

For example, consider Emma, who has a male colleague who often interrupts her during meetings. Emma recognizes that this behavior undermines her confidence and contributions. To address this, she decides to speak up during their next meeting. She calmly states, "I'd appreciate it if we could ensure that everyone has a chance to speak without interruptions." This assertion not only establishes her boundary but also fosters a culture of respect in their interactions.

Establishing Trust: The Foundation of Healthy Relationships

Trust is the cornerstone of any healthy relationship. It allows individuals to feel secure in their connections, enabling vulnerability and openness. For daughters who have grappled with the absence of paternal support, developing trust in male figures can be a complex process.

Recognizing the Role of Trust

Trust is built over time through consistent behavior and reliable communication. It involves the belief that the other person has one's best interests at heart and will act with integrity. For daughters, understanding that trust is a mutual endeavor is crucial. They must not only seek trust from others but also work to be trustworthy themselves.

Building Trust Through Consistency

One effective way to establish trust is through consistent actions. For example, if a daughter expresses a need for emotional support, she should follow through on her commitment to be present for others as well. This reciprocal approach creates a foundation of reliability.

Additionally, sharing small vulnerabilities can help in this process; as trust grows, daughters can gradually open up about deeper feelings and experiences.

In Sarah's journey, she found herself hesitant to trust her new partner due to past disappointments. To overcome this, she communicated her fears openly, explaining her struggles with trust. Her partner responded with understanding, assuring her that he would be patient and supportive as they navigated their relationship together. This commitment to building trust laid a strong foundation for their connection.

Practicing Emotional Vulnerability

Emotional vulnerability is often seen as a double-edged sword; it can lead to profound connection but also poses the risk of rejection. For daughters who have experienced father absence, embracing vulnerability may feel particularly challenging, as it often requires confronting fears of abandonment and disappointment.

Understanding Vulnerability as Strength

To practice emotional vulnerability, daughters must first reframe their understanding of vulnerability itself. Rather than viewing it as a weakness, they can recognize it as a strength that fosters authentic connections. By sharing fears, dreams, and insecurities, daughters invite others into their inner worlds, creating opportunities for empathy and understanding.

Creating Safe Spaces for Vulnerability

Creating a safe space is essential for vulnerability to flourish. This can be achieved by fostering an environment of non-judgment and active listening. When daughters engage with male figures who respect their feelings and provide support, they are more likely to feel comfortable sharing their vulnerabilities.

For instance, during a heart-to-heart conversation with her brother, Lily expressed her fears about not being good enough in her career. Rather than dismissing her concerns, her brother listened attentively and shared his own struggles, creating a bond rooted in mutual vulnerability. This exchange deepened their relationship and allowed Lily to feel heard and understood.

Navigating the Challenges of Vulnerability

While vulnerability can enrich relationships, it also comes with risks. Daughters may face moments of doubt or fear of being judged. Developing resilience in the face of vulnerability is crucial. This involves recognizing that not all experiences will lead to positive outcomes but that each attempt contributes to personal growth.

Building Resilience Through Reflection

After sharing vulnerable thoughts, daughters should take time to reflect on the experience. Did the conversation go as expected? What feelings arose during and after the discussion? By examining these emotions, daughters can build resilience and learn from their interactions.

For Claire, after an emotional conversation with a male friend, she initially felt exposed and anxious about how her vulnerability would be perceived. However, upon reflection, she realized that the openness had led to a deeper connection and an invitation for her friend to share his own experiences. This insight empowered her to embrace vulnerability in future interactions.

The Path to Healthy Relationships

Setting boundaries, establishing trust, and practicing emotional vulnerability are essential components of building healthy relationships with male figures. For daughters navigating the complexities of father absence, these elements can serve as powerful tools for healing and connection. By recognizing the importance of personal limits, engaging in open communication, and embracing vulnerability, daughters can cultivate relationships that are nurturing, respectful, and supportive.

As daughters continue on their journeys toward healthy relationships, they must remember that each step taken is an act of courage and self-discovery. The path may be fraught with challenges, but with intentional effort and self-compassion, daughters can rewrite their narratives and foster meaningful connections that reflect their true selves. Ultimately, this journey is not only about healing from past wounds but also about celebrating the possibilities of love, respect, and emotional intimacy in their future relationships.

Chapter 12:

Fathers in Modern Society

A. How Changing Family Structures Affect the Father-Daughter Relationship

The dynamics of family structures have undergone significant transformations in modern society, fundamentally reshaping the father-daughter relationship. These changes stem from various factors, including increased divorce rates, the rise of single-parent households, shifting gender roles, and evolving cultural norms. Understanding how these elements interact and influence the father-daughter bond is crucial for recognizing the multifaceted nature of contemporary fatherhood.

The Evolving Family Landscape

In recent decades, the traditional nuclear family model has given way to a more diverse range of family structures. The rise of single-parent families, blended families, and cohabiting couples has transformed how children, including daughters, experience parental relationships. In particular, daughters may face unique challenges in navigating their bonds with fathers within these varying contexts.

Single-Parent Households and Their Impact

The prevalence of single-parent households, often led by mothers, has changed the way daughters perceive and interact with their fathers. In instances where fathers are less involved, either due to separation or divorce, daughters may struggle with feelings of abandonment or confusion. The absence of a father figure can lead to emotional voids that impact daughters' self-esteem and their expectations of male relationships.

For instance, consider Mia, who grew up in a single-parent household after her parents divorced. Her father remained a sporadic presence in her life, visiting occasionally but lacking a consistent role. As Mia transitioned into adulthood, she found herself grappling with feelings of insecurity and an unfulfilled desire for paternal approval. These feelings often colored her interactions with male figures, making it challenging for her to establish trusting relationships.

Blended Families and Complicated Dynamics

In blended families, where children are raised by stepparents, the father-daughter relationship may take on new dimensions. Daughters may find themselves navigating complex feelings of loyalty and affection toward both their biological fathers and their stepparents. This duality can create emotional turbulence, particularly if the relationships with either figure are strained.

Take the case of Ava, who, after her mother remarried, was introduced to her stepfather. While Ava appreciated her stepfather's nurturing presence, she simultaneously felt a sense of loss regarding her biological father, who was less involved in her life after the divorce. As she attempted to balance her emotions, Ava learned the importance of open communication with both men, fostering relationships that acknowledged her unique feelings about each parental figure.

Shifting Gender Roles and Expectations

The modern fatherhood landscape is characterized by evolving gender roles and societal expectations. Increasingly, fathers are encouraged to take active roles in their daughters' lives, challenging the traditional image of fathers as distant providers. This shift can positively influence the father-daughter relationship, as more fathers seek to engage emotionally and participate in their daughters' upbringing.

The Importance of Involved Fatherhood

Research has shown that involved fathers contribute significantly to their daughters' emotional and psychological well-being. Daughters with actively engaged fathers tend to exhibit higher self-esteem, better academic performance, and healthier interpersonal relationships. These positive outcomes stem from fathers modeling behaviors such as empathy, communication, and problem-solving.

For example, Jake, a father of two daughters, made a conscious decision to prioritize involvement in their lives. He attended their school events, actively listened to their concerns, and encouraged their interests. As a result, his daughters flourished emotionally and academically, developing a strong bond with their father that fostered mutual respect and understanding.

Challenging Traditional Masculinity

In contrast, traditional views of masculinity that emphasize emotional stoicism can hinder fathers from connecting deeply with their daughters. Some fathers may struggle to express vulnerability or affection, leading to emotional gaps in the relationship. Recognizing the importance of emotional openness can help fathers break free from these constraints, allowing them to foster deeper connections with their daughters.

Consider the journey of Tom, who grew up with a father who rarely expressed emotions. When Tom became a father himself, he recognized the limitations of this approach. Determined to create a different experience for his daughter, he actively practiced emotional expression, encouraging her to share her feelings openly. This shift not only strengthened their bond but also empowered Tom's daughter to navigate her emotions more effectively.

Cultural Norms and Diversity

Cultural backgrounds play a significant role in shaping family dynamics and, consequently, father-daughter relationships. Different cultures may emphasize varying expectations of fatherhood, influencing how daughters perceive their fathers and the nature of their interactions. In some cultures, fathers may be seen as authority figures, while in others, they may take on more nurturing roles.

Understanding Cultural Influences

In cultures where patriarchal norms are dominant, daughters may experience pressure to conform to traditional gender roles, which can impact their relationships with fathers. These dynamics can lead to tension if daughters seek to challenge these roles or assert their independence.

For instance, Sofia, a daughter from a conservative background, faced challenges when pursuing her dream of becoming an artist, a career path that her father deemed unconventional. The conflict between Sofia's aspirations and her father's expectations created a rift in their relationship. Through open discussions, Sofia gradually helped her father understand her passion, allowing them to rebuild their connection based on mutual respect.

Embracing Diversity in Fatherhood

As society becomes increasingly diverse, the definition of fatherhood continues to evolve. LGBTQ+ families, adoptive parents, and varied family configurations bring new perspectives to the father-daughter relationship. These diverse experiences can enrich daughters' understanding of love, support, and familial bonds, allowing them to form connections based on authenticity rather than traditional norms.

For example, Lisa, raised by two mothers, had the unique opportunity to experience love and support from multiple parental figures. Her upbringing taught her to appreciate emotional openness and the importance of non-traditional family structures. As Lisa entered adulthood, she sought to cultivate relationships built on mutual respect, regardless of gender norms.

A New Era of Father-Daughter Relationships

Changing family structures significantly impact the father-daughter relationship in modern society. As single-parent households, blended families, and evolving gender roles shape the landscape of fatherhood, daughters must navigate these dynamics with resilience and openness. Recognizing the importance of active involvement, emotional expression, and cultural understanding can empower both fathers and daughters to forge connections that are nurturing, supportive, and transformative.

As society continues to evolve, it is essential to acknowledge that the father-daughter relationship is not defined by traditional norms but by the commitment to understanding, respect, and love. By fostering these values, fathers and daughters can build bonds that transcend the challenges posed by changing family structures, creating a foundation for healthier, more fulfilling relationships. Through open communication, emotional vulnerability, and a willingness to embrace diversity, the father-daughter relationship can thrive in this new era of fatherhood.

B. Examining the Social, Cultural, and Economic Pressures on Fatherhood Today

Fatherhood in modern society is a complex tapestry woven from various social, cultural, and economic threads. These pressures not only shape the expectations and experiences of fathers but also influence the overall dynamics within families. Understanding these multifaceted pressures is crucial for recognizing the challenges fathers face and the implications for their relationships with their children, especially their daughters.

Social Pressures: The Role of Masculinity

At the heart of the modern fatherhood experience lies a significant social pressure tied to prevailing notions of masculinity. Traditional views often associate masculinity with strength, stoicism, and financial provision. These expectations can create an overwhelming burden for fathers who feel they must embody these traits to be considered "good" dads. As societal norms evolve, the definition of masculinity is also shifting; however, many fathers still grapple with conflicting messages about what it means to be a man and a parent.

The Struggle with Emotional Expression

Fathers are often conditioned to suppress their emotions, viewing vulnerability as a sign of weakness. This cultural narrative can prevent them from forming deep emotional connections with their children, particularly their daughters, who often seek emotional intimacy and communication. For instance, consider James, a father who grew up in a household where showing emotion was frowned upon. Despite his desire to connect with his daughter on a deeper level, he struggled to express his feelings, leading to misunderstandings and distance between them. This internal conflict exemplifies the struggle many

163

fathers face as they attempt to navigate the delicate balance between traditional masculine ideals and the emotional needs of their children.

Peer Comparisons and Social Media Influences

In today's digital age, fathers are increasingly exposed to the curated lives of others through social media. The constant barrage of images depicting "ideal" fatherhood can intensify feelings of inadequacy and self-doubt. Fathers may find themselves comparing their parenting styles, financial successes, or family dynamics to those portrayed online, leading to anxiety and stress. The pressure to conform to these often unrealistic standards can hinder fathers from appreciating their unique parenting journey, leaving them feeling isolated and overwhelmed.

Cultural Pressures: Diversity and Expectation

Cultural norms significantly shape the expectations placed on fathers, with varying implications based on ethnicity, socioeconomic status, and regional differences. In some cultures, fatherhood is associated with strict authority and control, while others may emphasize emotional involvement and nurturing. As society becomes more diverse, fathers must navigate a landscape that often contains conflicting cultural messages about their roles.

The Impact of Cultural Expectations

Fathers from immigrant backgrounds may face additional pressures to uphold cultural traditions while adapting to new societal norms. For instance, a father of Hispanic descent might feel compelled to adhere to the cultural expectation of being a strong patriarch while also wanting to engage in a more emotionally expressive relationship with his daughter. This duality can lead to confusion and internal conflict as he strives to balance these cultural expectations with his desire to foster a nurturing and supportive environment.

Navigating Gender Roles in Diverse Families

Furthermore, the increasing visibility of LGBTQ+ families has broadened the understanding of fatherhood beyond traditional gender roles. For instance, same-sex couples raising children may face societal scrutiny or prejudice, leading to additional pressures on their parenting styles. Fathers in these families often have to confront external biases while simultaneously establishing their unique identities as parents. The journey of fathers in diverse family structures highlights the importance of understanding and validating varied experiences of fatherhood.

Economic Pressures: The Weight of Financial Responsibility

In addition to social and cultural pressures, economic factors play a significant role in shaping modern fatherhood. Many fathers today face the daunting challenge of providing for their families in a rapidly changing economic landscape. The rising costs of living, student debt, and stagnant wages can create stress and anxiety, affecting their ability to engage fully in their children's lives.

The Burden of Financial Provision

The expectation to be the primary breadwinner can weigh heavily on fathers, often leading to long hours at work and less time spent with their children. For example, Robert, a father of three, found himself working multiple jobs to make ends meet. While he wanted to be an involved parent, the demands of his job left him with little energy or time to connect with his daughters. This economic pressure can create a cycle of absenteeism, where fathers become physically present but emotionally distant due to work-related stress.

Job Insecurity and Its Emotional Toll

In today's economy, job insecurity adds another layer of complexity. With the rise of gig work and the decline of stable employment opportunities, many fathers face the anxiety of not knowing if they will be able to provide for their families. This uncertainty can lead to emotional strain that affects their interactions with their children. A father like Tom, who is juggling freelance jobs, may struggle to maintain a consistent presence in his children's lives, leading to feelings of guilt and inadequacy.

The Interplay of Pressures: Striving for Balance

These social, cultural, and economic pressures often intersect, creating a challenging environment for fathers trying to establish healthy relationships with their daughters. The struggle to embody traditional masculinity while embracing emotional vulnerability, the need to navigate diverse cultural expectations, and the financial burdens can leave fathers feeling overwhelmed and disconnected.

Seeking Support and Community

Recognizing these pressures is the first step toward alleviating their effects. Fathers must find supportive communities where they can share their experiences, challenges, and triumphs. Support groups, parenting classes, and online forums can provide valuable resources for fathers seeking to navigate their roles in a positive and affirming way.

For example, a local father's group might meet weekly to discuss challenges and share advice, fostering a sense of camaraderie and understanding among participants. This type of support can help fathers feel less isolated, encouraging them to embrace their vulnerabilities and redefine their roles within their families.

Reimagining Fatherhood for Future Generations

Ultimately, addressing the pressures on fatherhood today requires a societal shift in how we perceive and support fathers. By fostering open discussions about masculinity, recognizing the diversity of fatherhood experiences, and promoting work-life balance, we can create an environment that empowers fathers to embrace their roles wholeheartedly.

As fathers begin to break free from outdated expectations and reclaim their identities, they can foster stronger, more meaningful connections with their daughters. This shift not only benefits individual families but also contributes to healthier communities where fatherhood is seen as a rich, multifaceted experience rather than a rigid set of expectations.

Navigating the Complex Landscape of Fatherhood

The pressures surrounding fatherhood in modern society are complex and multifaceted, encompassing social, cultural, and economic dimensions. As fathers navigate these challenges, they must recognize the importance of emotional connection, cultural understanding, and financial stability in fostering strong relationships with their daughters. By acknowledging and addressing these pressures, fathers can cultivate a more enriching and fulfilling experience for themselves and their families, paving the way for healthier dynamics that transcend generational boundaries.

Chapter 13:

Supporting Father-Daughter Relationships

A. Encouraging Healthy Father Involvement in Various Family Settings

In the intricate dynamics of family life, the father-daughter relationship stands as a vital pillar that influences emotional, psychological, and social development. Encouraging healthy father involvement in various family settings is not just beneficial for daughters; it enriches the entire family structure, fostering resilience, emotional intelligence, and a sense of security. As societal expectations evolve, understanding the multifaceted role fathers play and promoting their active participation in parenting becomes increasingly essential.

The Importance of Active Fatherhood

The role of a father in a daughter's life extends far beyond the traditional boundaries of financial provision. Research consistently shows that involved fathers contribute positively to their children's development. Daughters with engaged fathers tend to exhibit higher self-esteem, improved academic performance, and better emotional regulation. Active fatherhood helps girls navigate challenges, develop healthy relationships, and understand their worth in a world that often imposes unrealistic standards.

For example, consider the story of Emily, a young girl who struggles with self-doubt and body image issues. Her father, Tom, makes a conscious effort to be present in her life - attending her dance recitals, engaging in meaningful conversations, and actively supporting her interests. As a result, Emily grows up with a solid sense of self-worth and confidence, significantly influenced by her father's unwavering support and involvement.

Fostering Engagement in Different Family Structures

As society embraces diverse family structures - ranging from single-parent households to blended families - the importance of father involvement becomes even more pronounced. Each family setting presents unique challenges and opportunities for fostering strong father-daughter relationships.

Single-Parent Families

In single-parent families, where fathers may not reside with their daughters full-time, maintaining a strong connection is crucial. Fathers in these situations can leverage technology to stay engaged, utilizing video calls, text messaging, and social media to create a consistent presence in their daughters' lives. For instance, James, a divorced father, sets aside time each week for a virtual "daddy-daughter date" where they watch a movie together or engage in a video game. This practice not only strengthens their bond but also reassures his daughter of his unwavering love and support.

Blended Families

In blended families, where children may have stepparents or siblings from previous relationships, fathers face the challenge of integrating into a new family dynamic. Open communication and mutual respect among all family members are essential for fostering a healthy environment. Fathers can encourage positive relationships by actively engaging with their daughters and promoting family activities that emphasize connection and fun. For example, a father in a blended family might organize weekly game nights that include both biological and stepchildren, helping to cultivate a sense of belonging and unity.

Cultural Considerations

Cultural context also plays a significant role in shaping father involvement. In many cultures, traditional gender roles dictate that fathers may be less emotionally expressive or engaged in nurturing roles. However, as societies evolve, the importance of emotional availability and participation becomes increasingly recognized. Fathers from diverse cultural backgrounds can work to bridge the gap between traditional expectations and modern parenting by being proactive in expressing love, affection, and support for their daughters.

Consider the example of Ahmed, a father from a culture that traditionally emphasizes authority over emotional connection. Recognizing the changing dynamics in society, he actively works to demonstrate love and support through simple gestures - like attending his daughter's school events or engaging in open conversations about her interests. This effort not only strengthens their bond but also encourages his daughter to embrace her identity confidently.

Strategies for Encouraging Healthy Father Involvement

Promoting healthy father involvement requires intentional strategies that support fathers in navigating their roles effectively. These strategies can be implemented at various levels, from individual families to community initiatives.

1. Education and Awareness Programs

Educational programs that highlight the importance of father involvement can help break down stereotypes and encourage fathers to take an active role in their daughters' lives. Workshops and seminars focusing on effective communication, emotional expression, and the impact of involved fatherhood can provide valuable tools for fathers seeking to enhance their relationships with their daughters.

For instance, community organizations can host seminars that bring fathers together to discuss challenges and share best practices. This creates a supportive environment where fathers can learn from each other and develop skills to foster healthy relationships.

2. Family-Friendly Policies

Society plays a critical role in shaping father involvement through family-friendly policies that promote work-life balance. Employers can offer flexible work schedules, paternity leave, and parental support programs that empower fathers to engage actively in their daughters' lives. When fathers have the opportunity to prioritize family, they are more likely to develop strong connections with their children.

For example, companies that provide parental leave allow fathers to be present during important milestones, such as the birth of a child or the early years of a daughter's life. This investment in family well-being contributes to healthier father-daughter relationships.

3. Community Support Systems

Creating community support systems that encourage father involvement can also make a significant impact. Mentorship programs, father support groups, and community events that celebrate fatherhood can foster a culture of engagement. Fathers who feel supported by their communities are more likely to invest time and effort into their relationships with their daughters.

For instance, a local community center might offer activities specifically designed for fathers and daughters, such as sports events or arts and crafts workshops. These events not only strengthen their bond but also provide opportunities for fathers to connect with other dads, fostering a sense of camaraderie and shared experiences.

The Role of Mothers in Supporting Father Involvement

While the focus is often on fathers, mothers play a vital role in facilitating and supporting healthy father involvement. Encouraging fathers to be present and engaged can lead to more harmonious family dynamics and emotional stability for children.

1. Promoting Open Communication

Mothers can promote open communication between fathers and daughters, emphasizing the importance of their relationship. Encouraging daughters to express their feelings about their fathers fosters understanding and connection.

For example, a mother might encourage her daughter to share her thoughts about her relationship with her father, providing a safe space for dialogue. This practice not only empowers daughters to voice their feelings but also helps fathers understand their daughters' needs better.

2. Supporting Shared Responsibilities

In dual-parent households, mothers can support shared parenting responsibilities, allowing fathers to take an active role in their daughters' lives. By sharing tasks such as homework help, extracurricular activities, and household duties, fathers are given more opportunities to engage with their daughters meaningfully.

For instance, a mother might suggest that her husband attend a dance recital while she handles other responsibilities, reinforcing the idea that both parents are equally invested in their daughter's life.

Nurturing Lifelong Bonds

Encouraging healthy father involvement in various family settings is essential for fostering strong, resilient father-daughter relationships. As societal norms continue to shift, it is imperative to support fathers in navigating their roles and embracing the profound impact they have on their daughters' lives. By promoting active engagement through education, community support, and shared responsibilities, we can cultivate an environment where fathers feel empowered to be present, nurturing, and emotionally available.

Ultimately, investing in father involvement is an investment in the emotional well-being of future generations. When fathers actively participate in their daughters' lives, they not only enrich their daughters' experiences but also contribute to healthier families and stronger communities. As we nurture these vital bonds, we pave the way for a future where every daughter can flourish with the unwavering support of a dedicated father.

B. Resources and Programs for Fathers and Daughters to Strengthen Bonds

In an age where the importance of familial relationships is increasingly recognized, resources and programs designed to strengthen the bond between fathers and daughters are more vital than ever. These initiatives not only provide opportunities for shared experiences but also foster emotional connections that can last a lifetime. With a variety of resources available, from community-based programs to online platforms, fathers and daughters can access the support they need to cultivate a healthy and enriching relationship.

Community-Based Programs

Local community organizations often serve as hubs for family-oriented activities that encourage father-daughter bonding. These programs can vary widely, offering a diverse array of experiences tailored to different interests and age groups.

1. Family Activity Nights

Many community centers host family activity nights that feature games, crafts, and workshops specifically designed for fathers and daughters. These events encourage playful interaction and collaboration, allowing families to create lasting memories together. For instance, a community center might organize a monthly game night where fathers and daughters can compete in board games, engage in team-building exercises, or work together on creative projects. Such environments promote camaraderie and open communication, essential elements in building a strong relationship.

2. Outdoor Adventure Programs

Outdoor adventure programs offer a unique opportunity for fathers and daughters to bond through shared physical activities. These programs often include hiking, camping, rock climbing, or nature exploration, allowing participants to step out of their comfort zones while supporting each other. For example, a local organization might offer weekend camping trips where fathers and daughters can learn survival skills, set up tents, and explore the wilderness together. These experiences build trust and resilience, as both parties rely on each other for support and encouragement.

3. Mentorship Programs

Mentorship programs provide structured opportunities for fathers and daughters to connect with one another while developing essential life skills. These programs may pair fathers with their daughters' friends or involve larger community-based mentorship initiatives. Through workshops and group activities, participants learn from one another while fostering a supportive atmosphere. A program might include guest speakers, skill-building sessions, and discussion forums where fathers and daughters can share their thoughts and experiences. Such mentorship opportunities not only strengthen the father-daughter bond but also allow for broader community engagement.

Educational Workshops and Seminars

Educational workshops and seminars focused on parenting can also play a crucial role in strengthening father-daughter relationships. These sessions often cover topics ranging from communication strategies to conflict resolution, providing fathers with valuable tools to navigate their roles effectively.

1. Parenting Skills Workshops

Workshops designed to enhance parenting skills can help fathers understand the unique dynamics of father-daughter relationships. These workshops often include expert-led discussions on emotional intelligence, active listening, and the significance of being present. Fathers are encouraged to share their experiences, fostering an open dialogue about the challenges and triumphs of parenting. For example, a local organization might host a series of workshops where fathers learn how to approach sensitive topics with their daughters, promoting healthy communication and emotional connection.

2. Emotional Intelligence Training

Emotional intelligence training can equip fathers with the skills necessary to understand and manage their emotions while empathizing with their daughters' feelings. Such training emphasizes the importance of emotional availability and vulnerability in fostering meaningful relationships. Fathers may engage in role-playing exercises and group discussions to practice expressing their feelings and responding to their daughters' emotional needs. This approach not only improves father-daughter communication but also encourages daughters to embrace their emotional landscape.

Online Resources and Platforms

The digital age has ushered in a wealth of online resources that fathers and daughters can utilize to enhance their relationship. From virtual workshops to social media communities, the internet provides numerous avenues for connection and support.

1. Virtual Workshops and Webinars

Numerous organizations and professionals offer virtual workshops and webinars that cover a wide range of topics related to father-daughter relationships. These sessions allow fathers to access valuable information and resources from the comfort of their homes. Topics may include effective communication, bonding activities, and the impact of active fatherhood on daughters' development. For instance, a parenting expert might host a live webinar where fathers can ask questions and receive tailored advice on navigating common parenting challenges.

2. Online Support Groups

Online support groups serve as valuable platforms where fathers can connect with one another, share their experiences, and seek advice. These communities foster a sense of belonging and provide a space for fathers to discuss their unique challenges and victories in parenting. Websites and social media groups dedicated to fatherhood offer forums for discussion, resource sharing, and emotional support. Engaging with peers in this manner allows fathers to learn from one another while reinforcing their commitment to being actively involved in their daughters' lives.

3. Parenting Blogs and Podcasts

The rise of parenting blogs and podcasts has created an extensive repository of information on various aspects of fatherhood. These platforms often feature expert advice, personal stories, and practical tips that fathers can apply in their relationships with their daughters. A blog may offer articles on understanding the developmental stages of daughters or navigating the challenges of adolescence, while a podcast might feature interviews with fathers sharing their experiences and insights. Engaging with such resources can inspire fathers to explore new ways to connect with their daughters.

Promoting Positive Role Models

Encouraging positive male role models is another essential component of strengthening father-daughter relationships. Fathers can benefit from observing and interacting with other engaged dads, learning from their experiences and perspectives.

1. Father-Daughter Events

Hosting father-daughter events, such as dance nights, picnics, or sports tournaments, can create opportunities for fathers to meet one another and share experiences. These gatherings foster a sense of community and encourage positive role modeling, as fathers witness firsthand the importance of engagement and emotional connection. For example, a community might organize an annual father-daughter dance, where fathers can witness other dads actively participating in their daughters' lives while enjoying a night of fun and bonding.

2. Sharing Stories of Fatherhood

Highlighting stories of positive fatherhood in media and community settings can inspire and motivate fathers to actively engage with their daughters. By showcasing successful father-daughter relationships, organizations can reinforce the idea that involved fatherhood leads to enriched lives for both fathers and daughters.

For instance, a local newspaper might feature a weekly column dedicated to showcasing father-daughter duos who engage in various activities, from volunteering together to pursuing shared hobbies. These stories serve as powerful reminders of the impact of active involvement and encourage fathers to seek out opportunities to connect with their daughters.

The Path to Stronger Bonds

In an ever-evolving society, the resources and programs available for fathers and daughters play a critical role in fostering healthy relationships. By participating in community-based initiatives, educational workshops, online platforms, and events that promote positive male role models, fathers can strengthen their bonds with their daughters in meaningful and lasting ways.

As fathers embrace the opportunities provided by these resources, they contribute not only to their daughters' emotional well-being but also to the broader fabric of society. The commitment to nurturing father-daughter relationships ultimately paves the way for future generations to experience the profound benefits of active and involved fatherhood, ensuring that every daughter has the support she needs to thrive.

Conclusion:

Moving from Absence to Empowerment

A. Reflecting on the Journey from the Pain of Father Absence to the Empowerment of Healing

The journey from the pain of father absence to the empowerment of healing is one that many individuals traverse, often marked by profound emotional complexities and significant personal growth. This journey encapsulates the struggle against the shadows of abandonment, the process of confronting and understanding one's emotional wounds, and ultimately, the transformation into a resilient individual who embraces the power of self-love and healing. It is a journey that necessitates introspection, support, and a commitment to personal development, culminating in the realization that one's past does not dictate their future.

Acknowledging the Pain of Absence

At the outset of this journey, the pain of father absence can feel overwhelming, often manifesting as feelings of inadequacy, abandonment, and a longing for connection. Daughters may grapple with the lingering effects of their father's absence, struggling to understand the emotional void it creates. This absence can result in deep-seated wounds that influence self-esteem, relationships, and emotional well-being. Acknowledging this pain is crucial, as it allows individuals to validate their experiences and recognize the impact of their father's absence on their lives. It is through this acknowledgment that they can begin to peel back the layers of hurt, revealing the deeper emotions and needs that lie beneath.

The Path of Healing

As the journey progresses, the focus shifts toward healing. This phase is characterized by a commitment to understanding and addressing the emotional wounds inflicted by father absence. Healing is not a linear process; it involves moments of reflection, confrontation, and sometimes regression. Therapeutic approaches such as counseling, journaling, and self-awareness exercises can serve as essential tools for individuals seeking to navigate this complex terrain. Counseling provides a safe space for exploring emotions and developing coping strategies, while journaling encourages personal reflection and self-discovery. Self-awareness exercises foster a deeper understanding of one's thoughts and behaviors, enabling individuals to break free from negative patterns rooted in their past.

The importance of community and support cannot be understated during this phase. Connecting with others who share similar experiences can provide a sense of belonging and understanding. Support groups, workshops, and community programs designed for individuals dealing with father absence offer opportunities for shared experiences, emotional validation, and the cultivation of new perspectives. Engaging in these supportive environments empowers individuals to voice their struggles, gain insights from others, and foster connections that reinforce their healing journey.

Embracing Empowerment

Ultimately, the journey leads to a place of empowerment, where individuals reclaim their narratives and redefine their identities beyond their father's absence. Empowerment is marked by a profound shift in mindset, where pain transforms into strength, and vulnerability becomes a source of resilience. Individuals learn to embrace self-love and recognize their worth independent of past experiences. This newfound empowerment is not merely an absence of pain but an active choice to pursue personal growth, establish healthy boundaries, and cultivate meaningful relationships.

Central to this empowerment is the process of forgiveness - both of oneself and of the absent father. Forgiveness does not imply condoning past actions but rather releasing the grip of resentment that can hinder healing. It allows individuals to free themselves from the emotional burdens tied to their father's absence, creating space for growth and new possibilities. This journey teaches that forgiveness is a personal choice that leads to emotional liberation, enabling individuals to move forward with a lighter heart.

The Journey Forward

As individuals emerge from the shadows of father absence, they carry with them valuable lessons learned along the way. They develop a deeper understanding of their emotional needs, cultivate healthier relationships, and embrace their roles as empowered individuals. The journey from pain to empowerment is a testament to resilience, illustrating that while father absence may leave a mark, it does not define one's destiny. Instead, it can serve as a catalyst for transformation - a powerful reminder that healing is possible, and that one can emerge stronger, wiser, and more capable of creating fulfilling connections.

In reflecting on this journey, it becomes clear that moving from absence to empowerment is not a destination but an ongoing process. It invites continuous self-discovery, growth, and a commitment to nurturing oneself and others. By embracing their stories and acknowledging the lessons learned, individuals not only heal themselves but also inspire those around them to embark on their own journeys of empowerment. This shared narrative becomes a beacon of hope, illuminating the path for future generations who may face similar challenges, reminding them that the journey from absence to empowerment is not only possible but also profoundly transformative.

B. How Daughters of Absent Fathers Can Thrive Despite the Emotional Setbacks

For daughters of absent fathers, the journey from pain to empowerment is often fraught with emotional challenges and setbacks. However, it is entirely possible for these daughters to not only survive but thrive, transforming their past experiences into a source of strength and resilience. This transformation is characterized by a combination of self-awareness, supportive relationships, and proactive strategies aimed at fostering personal growth and emotional well-being. By embracing their stories and utilizing the tools available to them, daughters can carve out fulfilling lives that are rich in meaning and purpose.

Embracing Self-Awareness

One of the foundational steps toward thriving after the absence of a father is cultivating self-awareness. This involves recognizing the ways in which father absence has impacted emotional well-being, behavior, and interpersonal relationships. Understanding these effects allows daughters to identify their emotional triggers and work through their feelings rather than being overwhelmed by them. Engaging in reflective practices, such as journaling or mindfulness, can aid in this process. Journaling provides a safe space to articulate thoughts and emotions, while mindfulness encourages living in the present moment, reducing anxiety about the past or future. This self-awareness fosters a deeper understanding of one's emotional landscape, empowering daughters to respond to challenges with insight and intentionality.

Building a Supportive Network

In navigating the complexities of life after father absence, the importance of a strong support network cannot be overstated. Daughters can benefit immensely from seeking relationships that offer emotional support, understanding, and validation. These relationships can take many forms - friends, mentors, teachers, or therapists - each providing unique perspectives and encouragement. Support groups specifically designed for individuals dealing with parental absence can also be invaluable, allowing daughters to connect with peers who share similar experiences. This sense of community can help alleviate feelings of isolation and foster a sense of belonging. By surrounding themselves with empathetic individuals, daughters can cultivate an environment that promotes healing and growth.

Developing Coping Strategies

Thriving despite emotional setbacks requires the development of effective coping strategies. These strategies can take various forms, including healthy lifestyle choices, stress management techniques, and goal-setting practices. Engaging in regular physical activity, for example, can have profound effects on mental health, as exercise releases endorphins - natural mood lifters that reduce stress and anxiety. Additionally, adopting a balanced diet and prioritizing sleep can enhance overall well-being, providing the physical energy needed to tackle emotional challenges.

Stress management techniques, such as deep breathing exercises, meditation, and yoga, can also play a crucial role in navigating emotional turbulence. These practices help to center the mind and body, promoting relaxation and emotional resilience. By equipping themselves with these coping mechanisms, daughters can face adversity with greater confidence and adaptability, transforming potential setbacks into opportunities for growth.

Pursuing Personal Goals

Thriving after the experience of father absence often involves setting and pursuing personal goals. Daughters can channel their energy into identifying what truly matters to them, whether that be academic achievements, career aspirations, creative pursuits, or community involvement. This focus on personal growth not only provides a sense of purpose but also reinforces a positive self-identity. Each goal achieved serves as a testament to resilience and determination, reinforcing the belief that they are capable of overcoming obstacles.

Engaging in activities that bring joy and fulfillment can also help daughters cultivate a sense of self-worth. Whether it's volunteering, pursuing a passion, or exploring new interests, these experiences enrich their lives and foster a strong sense of agency. By taking charge of their narratives and actively participating in shaping their futures, daughters reclaim their power and redefine their identities beyond their father's absence.

Embracing Forgiveness and Self-Love

Finally, an essential aspect of thriving is learning to embrace forgiveness - both of oneself and of the absent father. Forgiveness is not about condoning past actions but rather about freeing oneself from the burdens of resentment and anger. By letting go of these negative emotions, daughters create space for healing and growth. This process often requires time, reflection, and sometimes the guidance of a therapist.

Simultaneously, cultivating self-love is critical. Daughters must learn to acknowledge their worth and appreciate their unique qualities and strengths. Practicing self-compassion and positive affirmations can shift negative self-perceptions into empowering beliefs. By nurturing self-love, daughters can build a foundation of confidence that supports their journey toward thriving, allowing them to navigate life's challenges with grace and resilience.

Daughters of absent fathers can undoubtedly thrive despite the emotional setbacks they may face. By embracing self-awareness, building a supportive network, developing effective coping strategies, pursuing personal goals, and embracing forgiveness and self-love, they can transform their pain into empowerment. The journey is not without its difficulties, but the resilience cultivated through these experiences ultimately leads to a more profound understanding of oneself and a richer, more fulfilling life. It is a testament to the strength of the human spirit and the capacity for healing, reminding us that while the past may shape us, it does not define our futures. With determination and support, daughters can emerge as empowered individuals, ready to embrace the possibilities that lie ahead.

C. Hope for the Future: Using the Lessons of the Past to Build a Stronger Sense of Self

In the intricate tapestry of life, the absence of a father can leave profound emotional scars, yet it also offers invaluable lessons that can foster resilience and self-empowerment. Daughters who navigate this complex journey can find hope for the future by harnessing the wisdom gleaned from their past experiences. By reflecting on their struggles and triumphs, they can cultivate a stronger sense of self that empowers them to forge healthier relationships, pursue their dreams, and ultimately, lead fulfilling lives. This transformative process involves understanding the lessons of their past, redefining their narratives, and integrating these insights into their future aspirations.

Learning from the Past

The journey of self-discovery begins with an honest examination of one's past. Daughters of absent fathers often grapple with feelings of abandonment, inadequacy, and unresolved anger. Acknowledging these emotions is the first step toward healing. Understanding how these feelings have shaped their lives allows them to identify patterns of behavior that may hinder their progress. For instance, recognizing a tendency to seek validation from others or to avoid intimate relationships can illuminate areas in need of growth.

By transforming pain into insight, these daughters can reframe their narratives. Instead of seeing themselves solely as victims of circumstance, they can embrace their resilience and ability to overcome adversity. This shift in perspective lays the foundation for a stronger sense of self. Through this lens, the lessons of the past become stepping stones rather than stumbling blocks. Each experience, whether painful or joyful, contributes to the richness of their identity and offers opportunities for growth.

Redefining Identity

As daughters reflect on their past, they have the unique opportunity to redefine their identities. Often, the absence of a father figure can lead to a sense of incompleteness or a fractured self-image. However, this does not have to be the defining narrative. By actively engaging in self-reflection and self-affirmation, daughters can begin to construct a new identity that is independent of their father's absence.

This process involves identifying personal values, strengths, and passions. Daughters can explore various aspects of themselves, from their interests to their talents, and learn to appreciate their individuality. Embracing their uniqueness allows them to break free from the constraints of societal expectations and the burdens of their past. By crafting a positive self-image rooted in self-acceptance, they can cultivate a sense of empowerment that propels them forward.

Building Resilience

Resilience is a critical quality that daughters of absent fathers can cultivate through their experiences. The challenges they face, while daunting, can serve as powerful teachers. Each hurdle overcome becomes a testament to their strength and determination. By embracing resilience, daughters learn that setbacks do not define their futures; instead, they offer opportunities for growth and renewal.

This resilience can be further reinforced by setting realistic goals and celebrating small achievements along the way. Whether it's completing a personal project, advancing in a career, or nurturing healthy relationships, each success contributes to a growing sense of self-efficacy. This sense of accomplishment fuels hope for the future, fostering a belief that they can create the lives they envision for themselves.

Creating Healthy Relationships

The lessons learned from the past also inform how daughters approach relationships in the future. Having navigated the complexities of father absence, they are equipped with a unique understanding of the importance of emotional connection and trust. As they cultivate healthy relationships with male figures and others in their lives, they can apply the insights gained from their experiences.

This journey involves establishing boundaries, practicing open communication, and seeking relationships that foster mutual respect and understanding. By modeling healthy dynamics, daughters can break the cycle of emotional pain that may have originated in their childhoods. This proactive approach not only strengthens their sense of self but also enhances their ability to form deep, meaningful connections.

Embracing Hope and Possibility

Ultimately, hope for the future lies in the ability to envision possibilities beyond the constraints of the past. Daughters of absent fathers can harness their experiences to create a brighter future filled with opportunities for growth and fulfillment. This hope is rooted in the understanding that they possess the tools to shape their lives and pursue their dreams.

Engaging in personal development, whether through education, creative expression, or community involvement, allows daughters to actively participate in their journeys. By seeking out new experiences and challenging themselves to step outside their comfort zones, they can expand their horizons and uncover latent potentials. The future becomes a canvas upon which they can paint their aspirations, fueled by the resilience and strength cultivated through their past.

The journey from absence to empowerment is one of transformation, resilience, and hope. Daughters of absent fathers have the unique opportunity to learn from their past experiences, redefining their identities and building a stronger sense of self. By embracing the lessons of the past, fostering resilience, and creating healthy relationships, they can move forward with confidence and purpose. Hope is not merely a passive feeling; it is an active force that drives them to seek fulfillment and joy in their lives. Ultimately, the future is theirs to shape, a testament to their strength, determination, and unwavering spirit. The echoes of their past serve not as chains but as wings, enabling them to soar to new heights of possibility and empowerment.

Additional Resources

A. Books, Articles, and Organizations that Support Daughters of Absent Fathers

Navigating the complexities of growing up with an absent father can be a challenging journey. Fortunately, numerous resources can provide support, guidance, and a sense of community for daughters seeking to understand and heal from their experiences. Here is a curated list of books, articles, and organizations that can serve as valuable tools in this process.

Books

1. **"The Fatherless Daughter Project: Understanding Our Losses and How to Move Forward" by Denizet-Lewis and Dr. L. A. K. F. Roberts**

   ✓ This insightful book dives deep into the experiences of daughters who have grown up without a father. It provides personal narratives and research, exploring how father absence affects various aspects of life, from relationships to self-esteem. It also offers practical advice on how to heal and move forward.

2. **"Daughters of Absent Fathers: A Journey Towards Wholeness" by Dr. Jennifer M. F. Armentrout**

   ✓ Dr. Armentrout's book focuses on the emotional and psychological impact of father absence on daughters. Through case studies and therapeutic approaches, she outlines steps for healing, emphasizing self-discovery and empowerment.

3. **"Healing the Father Wound: How to Create Healthy Relationships with Your Father and Others" by Heather M. Thomas**

   ✓ This book addresses the core issues related to father absence and its impact on relationships. It offers strategies for healing, including forgiveness and setting boundaries, helping readers understand the patterns that may have developed in their own lives.

4. **"The Gift of Fatherhood: A Guide for Daughters" by Sandra D. Webb**

   ✓ This guide highlights the positive aspects of father-daughter relationships and how daughters can cultivate healthy connections despite the absence. It encourages readers to find father figures and mentors in their lives while fostering self-love and resilience.

5. **"Not a Father's Day: A Daughter's Journey to Healing" by Lauren L. Fisher**

   ✓ A poignant memoir that chronicles the author's journey of growing up without a father. Fisher shares her struggles and triumphs, providing a relatable narrative that encourages healing and growth.

Articles

1. **"The Impact of Father Absence on Daughters" (Psychology Today)**

   ✓ This article examines the psychological effects of growing up without a father and offers insights into the long-term implications on emotional well-being, self-esteem, and relationship dynamics. It highlights the importance of addressing these challenges and seeking support.

2. **"Healing the Father Wound: Finding Your Voice as a Daughter" (HuffPost)**

   ✓ This article explores the concept of the "father wound" and how it manifests in various aspects of life. It provides practical advice on healing and encourages daughters to embrace their narratives and take ownership of their stories.

3. **"Daughters of Absent Fathers: Strategies for Healing" (Verywell Mind)**

   ✓ This resource outlines effective strategies for coping with the emotional pain associated with father absence. It emphasizes the importance of self-awareness, therapy, and community support in the healing process.

Organizations

1. **The Fatherless Daughters Network**

   ✓ This nonprofit organization provides support, resources, and community for daughters who have experienced father absence. They offer workshops, support groups, and online resources to help daughters navigate their healing journeys.

2. **Girl Scouts of the USA**

   ✓ While not specifically focused on father absence, the Girl Scouts offer programs that empower girls through mentorship and leadership development. They provide a supportive environment where daughters can build connections and gain confidence.

3. **The National Fatherhood Initiative**

✓ This organization focuses on promoting responsible fatherhood and strengthening father-child relationships. They offer resources and programs designed to encourage active and engaged fathering, providing valuable insights for daughters seeking to understand and improve their relationships with male figures.

4. **Mothers Against Drunk Driving (MADD)**

✓ MADD offers resources for children affected by the absence of a father due to addiction or tragic circumstances. Their programs support healing and resilience, focusing on community and shared experiences.

5. **BetterHelp**

✓ This online counseling platform connects individuals with licensed therapists who specialize in various issues, including father absence and emotional healing. The flexibility of online therapy makes it accessible to those seeking support on their journey.

The path toward healing and empowerment for daughters of absent fathers is deeply personal and often challenging. However, the resources outlined above can serve as valuable companions along this journey. Whether through books that offer wisdom, articles that provide insights, or organizations that foster community and support, daughters can find the guidance they need to navigate their emotions and build healthier, more fulfilling lives. By engaging with these resources, they can transform their experiences into opportunities for growth and resilience, ultimately creating a brighter future for themselves.

B. Therapeutic Practices and Support Groups

For daughters of absent fathers, engaging in therapeutic practices and participating in support groups can be transformative steps toward healing and empowerment. These avenues provide opportunities for self-exploration, emotional release, and connection with others who share similar experiences. Below is an exploration of effective therapeutic practices and notable support groups that can aid in the healing journey.

Therapeutic Practices

1. **Individual Counseling**

   ✓ **Overview:** Individual counseling allows for personalized support tailored to specific emotional needs. A licensed therapist can help daughters explore their feelings about father absence, process childhood wounds, and develop coping strategies.

   ✓ **Benefits:** Therapy provides a safe and confidential space to express feelings without judgment. Through guided conversations, daughters can gain insights into their behavior patterns, self-worth, and relationships.

2. **Group Therapy**

   ✓ **Overview:** Group therapy consists of small groups led by a trained therapist where individuals share their experiences and challenges. It offers a sense of community and collective healing.

   ✓ **Benefits:** Participants benefit from hearing diverse perspectives and learning from one another's experiences. The shared understanding fosters connection and reduces feelings of isolation.

3. **Art Therapy**

   ✓ **Overview:** Art therapy combines creative expression with psychological healing. Participants use various artistic mediums - painting, drawing, or sculpting - to explore their emotions.

   ✓ **Benefits:** Art can serve as a powerful outlet for feelings that are difficult to articulate. This non-verbal form of expression can lead to insights and breakthroughs, providing a pathway to healing.

4. **Mindfulness and Meditation**

   ✓ **Overview:** Mindfulness practices, including meditation and yoga, focus on being present in the moment and cultivating self-awareness. These practices can help individuals manage anxiety and emotional distress.

   ✓ **Benefits:** Mindfulness promotes relaxation and emotional regulation, allowing daughters to process their feelings related to father absence more effectively. It can also foster self-compassion and acceptance.

5. **Journaling**

   ✓ **Overview:** Journaling involves writing down thoughts and feelings as a form of self-reflection. This practice can be therapeutic and aid in understanding emotions and patterns.

   ✓ **Benefits:** Journaling encourages introspection and can help clarify feelings surrounding father absence. It provides a private space to express grief, anger, and hope, which can be cathartic and enlightening.

Support Groups

1. **Daughters of Absent Fathers Support Group**

   ✓ **Overview:** This specialized support group focuses on the unique experiences of daughters who have grown up without father figures. It offers a safe environment for sharing and connecting.

   ✓ **Activities:** Group members share stories, discuss challenges, and provide mutual support. Facilitators often include therapists who guide discussions and introduce coping strategies.

2. **The Fatherless Daughters Network**

   ✓ **Overview:** This organization offers both online and in-person support groups for daughters dealing with the effects of father absence. Their mission is to empower women through community and connection.

   ✓ **Activities:** Regular meetings and events provide opportunities for members to share their experiences, attend workshops, and participate in activities that promote healing.

3. **Online Support Communities**

   ✓ **Overview:** Numerous online forums and social media groups are dedicated to discussing the impacts of father absence. These platforms provide anonymity and a vast network of individuals with shared experiences.

   ✓ **Benefits:** Online communities can offer immediate support and resources, making it easy for individuals to engage from the comfort of their homes. Members can share articles, resources, and personal stories.

4. **Peer Support Programs**

✓ **Overview:** Peer support programs connect daughters with trained peers who have experienced similar challenges. These programs focus on shared experiences and encourage mutual understanding.

✓ **Benefits:** Peer support fosters a sense of belonging and reduces feelings of isolation. Daughters can find solace in connecting with others who understand their journeys and can offer empathy and encouragement.

5. **Workshops and Retreats**

✓ **Overview:** Various organizations offer workshops and retreats focused on healing from father absence. These immersive experiences provide participants with tools for personal growth and emotional healing.

✓ **Activities:** Workshops may include activities like group discussions, creative expression, and mindfulness exercises, all aimed at fostering community and healing.

Therapeutic practices and support groups play a crucial role in the healing journey for daughters of absent fathers. By engaging in individual and group therapy, participating in creative outlets, and connecting with others who understand their experiences, these daughters can navigate their emotions and foster resilience. The resources available, whether through professional guidance or peer support, empower them to break free from the past and embrace a future filled with hope, self-love, and personal growth. These avenues not only facilitate healing but also create a sense of community that is essential for ongoing support and connection.

C. Suggestions for Further Reading on Father-Daughter Dynamics

Understanding father-daughter dynamics is a multifaceted journey that encompasses emotional, psychological, and social dimensions. There is a wealth of literature that explores these relationships, offering insights into the challenges, triumphs, and transformative processes that shape them. Below are suggested readings that delve into various aspects of father-daughter relationships, providing valuable perspectives and practical advice for daughters navigating their unique experiences.

Books

1. **"Father-Daughter Relationships: Contemporary Research and Issues" by Dr. Linda Nielsen**

   ✓ **Overview:** This comprehensive book examines the complex dynamics between fathers and daughters from various angles, including psychological research, social changes, and personal narratives.

   ✓ **Key Themes:** The book covers the significance of paternal involvement, the impact of father absence, and the positive outcomes of healthy father-daughter relationships.

2. **"The Fatherless Daughter Project: Understanding Our Losses and Choosing to Live Fully" by Denise D. Shull**

   ✓ **Overview:** Drawing from her own experiences as a fatherless daughter, Shull presents a guide for women seeking to heal from the emotional wounds of father absence.

   ✓ **Key Themes:** The book emphasizes empowerment, personal growth, and the importance of creating a fulfilling life despite past challenges.

3. **"The Power of Dads: A Journey to Connect with Your Daughter" by Dr. Rick Johnson**

   ✓ **Overview:** This book is a heartfelt exploration of how fathers can nurture their daughters through meaningful relationships and open communication.

   ✓ **Key Themes:** It offers practical strategies for fathers aiming to foster strong emotional bonds and promote healthy development in their daughters.

4. **"Daughters of Dads: A Guide to Parenting Girls" by Dr. Susan D. T. Allen**

   ✓ **Overview:** This resource addresses the unique challenges fathers face in parenting daughters and provides actionable tips for effective communication and connection.

   ✓ **Key Themes:** The book highlights the critical role fathers play in their daughters' self-esteem and emotional well-being.

5. **"Healing the Father Wound: A Guide to Forgiveness and Self-Love" by Linda Shalowitz**

   ✓ **Overview:** Shalowitz's book offers a compassionate approach to understanding the impact of absent fathers and provides guidance for healing through forgiveness and self-compassion.

   ✓ **Key Themes:** It explores emotional healing, self-acceptance, and the journey towards reclaiming personal power.

Articles and Journals

1. **"The Impact of Father Absence on Daughters: A Review of the Literature"** - This scholarly article reviews various studies examining the psychological and social effects of father absence on

daughters, providing a comprehensive overview of the challenges they face.

✓ **Source:** Journal of Child Psychology and Psychiatry

2. **"Father-Daughter Relationships: An Important Factor in Female Development"** - This article discusses the critical role fathers play in the emotional and psychological development of their daughters and explores strategies for fostering healthy relationships.

✓ **Source:** Child Development Perspectives

3. **"Navigating the Father-Daughter Relationship: A Roadmap for Healing"** - A practical guide that offers insights into common issues faced by daughters with absent fathers, along with strategies for building healthier relationships.

✓ **Source:** Psychology Today

Online Resources and Websites

1. **The Fatherless Daughters Network (www.fatherlessdaughters.com)**

✓ **Overview:** This website offers a wealth of resources, including articles, personal stories, and information about support groups and events for women affected by father absence.

✓ **Key Features:** The network provides community forums, workshops, and events to foster connection and healing among members.

2. **The American Psychological Association (www.apa.org)**

✓ **Overview:** The APA offers numerous articles and resources on father-daughter dynamics, including research findings and practical advice for navigating these relationships.

✓ **Key Features:** The site includes links to studies, articles, and resources for mental health professionals and individuals seeking to understand father-daughter relationships better.

3. **Psychology Today (www.psychologytoday.com)**

   ✓ **Overview:** This magazine features a variety of articles exploring the complexities of father-daughter relationships, mental health, and emotional well-being.

   ✓ **Key Features:** Readers can find expert advice, personal narratives, and discussions on the psychological aspects of father absence and its effects on daughters.

The suggested readings and resources above offer valuable insights into the complexities of father-daughter dynamics. By engaging with these materials, daughters of absent fathers can deepen their understanding of their experiences, find validation, and discover pathways toward healing and empowerment. Whether through personal narratives, academic studies, or practical guides, the knowledge gained from these resources can be instrumental in navigating the challenges and triumphs of their relationships with their fathers and themselves. Each book and article serves as a stepping stone towards fostering healthier connections, breaking the cycle of pain, and ultimately embracing a future filled with hope and self-love.

Made in the USA
Las Vegas, NV
23 December 2024

15304883R00118